Japanese Educational System and its Administration

日本の教育制度と教育行政（英語版）

The Kansai Society for Educational Administration

関西教育行政学会 編

東信堂

Preface

The Kansai Society for Educational Administration (KSEA) was founded in 1957. It is older than the Japan Educational Administration Society and is the first academic society in Japan in this field. The society has held regular meetings almost every month for 60 years, longer than its foundation. Since 1970, annual bulletins have been issued, the latest one was published in March 2017. I am deeply grateful that such continuity is a result of the great efforts of past presidents and the understanding and support of all members.

From the spring of last year, the Board of Directors have been diligently working on the academic society's 60th anniversary commemoration project to publish an updated English textbook focused on Japanese education and its administration system. This type of publication was already published in September, 1999 commemorating the 40th anniversary of KSEA under the title "Educational System and Administration in Japan" (Kyodo Shuppan). At that time, Japan's internationalization began to progress in various areas including education. Therefore, the number of educators and researchers from abroad visiting schools and universities in Japan had dramatically increased. High quality information relating to Japan's education system was required and deepening international understanding was becoming indispensable for Japanese people.

Since then, international relations, and political and economic circumstances surrounding Japan have changed drastically. In addition, the international expansion of universities - especially those in China, Korea and Taiwan - has been rapid in recent years. Japanese universities tend to lag behind the wave of internationalization and must catch up with and surpass those which have advanced.

Also, global ranking of universities has been receiving a lot of attention in recent years and Japanese universities are struggling to raise their evaluations. The number of citations of papers submitted by Skorpath, etc. plays an important role in the evaluation. We cannot expect to improve the international ranking of Japanese universities without overcoming weaknesses in English firstly. Researchers of previous generation have only submitted papers to national or regional academic journals in Japanese. There are few cases of submitting papers, mainly in English, to foreign academic journals. It is necessary for the next generation to strengthen their international communication capabilities and acquire international correspondence skills. It is noteworthy that this publication project was timely and presents an opportunity for catalyzing such abilities. There is a tradition to nurture the next generation that transcends academic clique and guides our academic disciplines. It is a philosophy of our academic society that has been passed down since its incarnation. The planning of this publication is in line with such policy and will hopefully have great significance for the internationalization of educational administration as well. In addition, by writing this information in English, it is our intention that international readers can appreciate and gain a better understanding of modern education in Japan.

Members of the KSEA undertook the writing of every section. Former president of KSEA, Dr. UEDA, Manabu acted as editorial chairperson and performed many functions such as planning, organizing, and negotiating with a publisher. Dr. MURATA, Yokuo, Dr. TANIGAWA, Yoshitaka and Prof. NAMBU, Hatsuyo contributed as Editorial Committee Members and Associate Prof. MIYAMURA, Yuko contributed as editorial secretary.

Lastly, I would like to express my deepest gratitude to Mr. SHIMODA, Katsushi president of the Toshindo Publishing Company. He accepted this publication under very serious circumstances. I sincerely express my gratitude to everyone involved.

Professor TAKAMI, Shigeru
President of the Kansai Society for Educational Administration (KSEA)

本書の意義

　本書は関西教育行政学会が 1999 年に刊行した Educational System and Administration in japan の改訂版として、現代までの様々な制度改革や教育環境の変化等をふまえ、あらたに作成されたものである。

　21 世紀に入ってから現在にいたる 10 数年の間に訪日外国人数は 5 倍（政府観光局）にまでになり、この傾向は東京オリンピック・パラリンピック（2020）の開催を控えてさらに強まると予想される。訪日目的には短期的な旅行のほか、高等教育機関への留学あるいはビジネス、技術研修など長期滞在型も数多く見受けられる。日本の教育の実情や特徴などは日本を理解するうえで欠かせない一面であり、それらに関心をもつ訪日外国人が増えていることは否定できない。教育関係の出版物は数多いが、現代の教育制度や学校教育などについて、コンパクトにしかも英文でまとめたものは極めて少ない。その意味で本書は、英語での情報提供という意味で外国人にとって利便性が高いといえよう。

　他方、海外渡航する日本人の数には近年あまり大きな変化が見られないが、以前から海外への赴任、留学、調査、研究等で長期間現地に滞在する人は多い。外国では日本の教育への関心が比較的高く、「日本の教育の特徴」や「学校教育」など、日本の現状を尋ねられる場面は少なくない。このような場合、最新の情報に基づいて日本の教育全般にわたって英語で記述した本書は大いに役立つであろう。

　さらには外国人だけでなく、日本人が英語で日本の教育に関する文書を作る場面でも、基本的な教育用語はいうに及ばず、教育の各段階を通じて簡略に説明し、また現代の問題点や今後の方向を示唆した本書は、有力な素材となろう。

　本書が、上記のような多様なニーズに応えられれば、これに勝る喜びはない。

編集委員会代表
上田　学

Contents

Preface	3
Contributors	10
Abbreviations	12
List of Figures & Tables, etc.	13

Introduction: Background of Present Japanese Educational System 15

Part 1. Schools and Educational System
Chapter 1. Schools
§1. Early Childhood Education and Care	24
§2. Primary Education	32
*Column-1: One Day in Primary School	42
§3. Secondary Education	43
*Column-2: Special Activities	51
*Column-3: One Day in a Lower Secondary School	52
§4. Higher Education	53
§5. Special Needs Education	64
§6. Specialized Training College and Miscellaneous Schools	70
*Column-4: Cram schools	75

Chapter 2. Curriculum Standards	76
*Column-5: The System and Situation of Student Promotion in School	83
Chapter 3. School Management	84
Chapter 4. Teacher System	96
*Column-6: Lesson Study	108
Chapter 5. Private Schools	109

| Chapter 6. Social Education | 117 |
| *Column-7: Lifelong Education | 127 |

Part 2. Educational Administration

Chapter 7. Role of the State	130
Chapter 8. Local Educational Administration	142
Chapter 9. Educational Finance	159
*Column-8: School Facilities	169
Chapter 10. Features of Educational Administration in Japan	170

Part 3. Movement for Reform

Chapter 11. Reform of Compulsory Education	184
*Column-9: Absenteeism and Free school	191
Chapter 12. Secondary Education Reforms	192
*Column-10: Career Education	199
Chapter 13. Higher Education Reform	200
Chapter 14. Internationalization of Education	208
Chapter 15. Changing Political Process of Education Policy	217

Statistics	228
Further Readings	234
Chronology (1947–2016)	237
Useful Website	241

| Index | 242 |

| Editor's Postscript | 245 |

目　次

まえがき ……………………………………………… 3
執筆者一覧 …………………………………………… 10
略語集 ………………………………………………… 12
図表等一覧 …………………………………………… 13

序　日本の教育制度の基盤とその背景 ……………… 15

第1部　学校および教育制度
第1章　学校
　1節　就学前教育 ………………………………… 24
　2節　初等教育 …………………………………… 32
　　　コラム1　小学校の一日 …………………… 42
　3節　中等教育 …………………………………… 43
　　　コラム2　特別活動 ………………………… 51
　　　コラム3　中学校の一日 …………………… 52
　4節　高等教育 …………………………………… 53
　5節　特別支援教育 ……………………………… 64
　6節　専修学校・各種学校 ……………………… 70
　　　コラム4　学習塾 …………………………… 75
第2章　教育課程 ………………………………… 76
　　　コラム5　進級制度 ………………………… 83
第3章　学校経営 ………………………………… 84
第4章　教員制度 ………………………………… 96
　　　コラム6　授業研究 ………………………… 108
第5章　私立学校 ……………………………… 109
第6章　社会教育 ……………………………… 117
　　　コラム7　生涯教育 ………………………… 127

第2部　教育行政
　第7章　国の役割……………………………………… 130
　第8章　地方の教育行政……………………………… 142
　第9章　教育財政……………………………………… 159
　　　コラム8　学校の施設 …………………… 169
　第10章　日本の教育行政の特徴…………………… 170

第3部　教育改革の動向
　第11章　義務教育改革……………………………… 184
　　　コラム9　不登校・フリースクール …… 191
　第12章　中等教育改革……………………………… 192
　　　コラム10　キャリア教育 …………… 199
　第13章　高等教育改革……………………………… 200
　第14章　教育の国際化……………………………… 208
　第15章　教育政策過程の転換……………………… 217

基本統計…………………………………………………… 228
参考文献…………………………………………………… 234
年表………………………………………………………… 237
関係団体・組織へのアクセス………………………… 241
索引………………………………………………………… 242
あとがき…………………………………………………… 245

Contributors

TAKAMI, Shigeru (Kyoto University)　　　　　　　Preface

ASADA, Shohei (Shitennoji University)　　　　　Ch. 2

CHIKUSA, Tomoaki (Kyoto University of Education) Ch. 9

ENOKI, Keiko (Kyushu University)　　　　　　　Column-1

EGAMI, Naoki (University of Fukuchiyama)　　　Column-5

FURUTA, Kaori (Hyogo University)　　　　　　　Ch. 5

GUO, Xiaobo (Kyoto University)　　　　　　　　Appendix

HATTORI, Kenji (Kyoto University)　　　　　　　Ch. 1-4

HIRASAKA, Miho (Heian Jogakuin University)　　Ch. 1-2, 3

KANI, Mizuki (Nakakyushu Junior College)　　　Column-10

KIRIMURA,Takafumi (Kobe Tokiwa University)　 Ch. 1-3, 12

KONDO, Chizue (Kozu Upper Secondary School, Osaka Prefecture)

　　　　　　　　　　　　　　　　　　　　　　Ch. 1-3, 12

MIYAMURA, Yuko (Kio University)　　　　　　　Ch. 6

MIZUMORI, Yurika (Kyoto Women's University: PS) Ch. 1-2

MURATA, Yokuo (University of Tsukuba ★)　　　Ch.14, Column-2, 8

NAGATA, Eriko (Osaka City University ✻)　　　　Column-6

NAKAJIMA, Chie (Kyoto Bunkyo University)　　　Ch. 1-1

NAMBU, Hatsuyo (Nagoya University)　　　　　　Ch. 4

NISHIKAWA, Jun (Kyoto University ☆)　　　　　Appendix

NISHIKAWA, Nobuhiro (Kyoto Sangyo University) Ch. 11

NISHINO, Michiyo (Kobe University ☆)	Column-3
OHMURA, Kazumasa (Ritsumeikan University, PS)	Ch. 15
OHNO , Yasuki (Shiga University)	Ch. 3
OTANI, Susumu (University of Tsukuba)	Ch. 1-6
SHIBA, Takafumi (Poole Gakuin University)	Column-7
SUZUKI, Mariko (Ryutsu Keizai University)	Ch. 8
TAIRA, Tomoe (IC Net Limited.)	Ch. 14
TAKEI , Tetsuro (Ritsumeikan University)	Column-9
TAMURA, Noriko (Biwako Seikei Sport College)	Column-4
TANIGAWA, Yoshitaka (Kyoto Women's University)	Ch. 8
TANIMURA, Ayako (Senri Kinran University)	Ch. 1-5
UEDA, Manabu (Kyoto Women's University ★)	Introduction
UEDA, Satoshi (Nishikyushu University)	Ch. 14
YAMASHITA, Koichi (Kobe University)	Ch. 10
YONEHARA, Aki (Toyo University)	Ch. 7
YONEOKA, Yumi (Saitama Medical University)	Ch. 7
YOSHIDA, Takehiro (Kansai University of International Studies)	Ch. 13

★: Emeritus Professor
☆: Research Fellow of the Japan Society for the Promotion of Science
PS: Parttime Staff
✳: Research Fellow

Abbreviations

CCE   Central Council for Education（中央教育審議会）

CRE   Council for Revitalization of Education（教育再生実行会議）

ECEC   Early Childhood Education and Care（幼児教育・保育）

FLE   Fundamental Law of Education（教育基本法）

ICT   Information and Communication Technology（情報通信技術）

IEI   Incorporated Educational Institution（学校法人）

LCOOLEA Law concerning Organization and Operation of Local Educational Administration（地方教育行政の組織及び運営に関する法律）

MESSC   Ministry of Education, Sports, Science and Culture（文部省、1949 ～ 2001）

MEXT   Ministry of Education, Culture, Sports, Science and Technology（文部科学省、2001 ～）

MHLW   Ministry of Health, Labor and Welfare（厚生労働省）

NCER   National Commission on Educational Reform（教育改革国民会議）

NCTUA   National Center Test for University Admission（大学入学センター試験）

SEL   School Education Law（学校教育法）

List of Figures, Tables and Pictures

	No.	Title	page
Fig.	1-1	Percentage of Students for Post-compulsory Education	17
	1-2	Number of Newborn Babies	19
	1-3	Percentage of Children supported by Local Government Educational Aids	21
	1-1-1	ECEC Facilities in Japan	27
	1-3-1	Mental Health of Students	45
	1-3-2	Situation of Individual-based Teaching	46
	1-3-3	Situation of Individual-based Learning	46
	1-3-4	Contents of Career and Academic Counselling	47
	1-3-5	Number of Students by Upper Secondary School Courses	50
	1-6-1	Number of Specialized Training Colleges and Miscellaneous Schools	71
	1-6-2	The Number of Students in Specialized Training Colleges and Miscellaneous Schools	72
	2-1	Current Distribution System of Textbooks	79
	3-1	Organization of School Management (A Case of Lower Secondary School)	88
	6-1	Changes in the Number of Major Social Education Facilities	121
	7-1	Organization Chart of MEXT	133
	8-1	Structure of the Board of Education (before 2014)	147
	8-2	Structure of the Board of Education (after 2014)	149
	9-1	Public Expenditure on Education as Percentage of GDP	159
	9-2	Public Expenditure on Education in Total Expenditure	160
	12-1	Ratio of Students belonging to Extra-curricular Clubs	193
	12-2	Number of Secondary Education Schools	194
	14-1	The Number of Children who need Japanese Instruction	209
Table	1-1-1	Categories of ECEC Certification under the New System	26
	1-1-2	Desirable Growth by the End of Early Childhood	29
	1-2-1	Numbers of Each Subject in a Year (Primary School 2002-)	36
	1-2-2	One Day in Primary School	42
	1-3-1	Numbers of Each Subject in Lower Secondary School (2008)	44
	1-3-2	One Day in Lower Secondary School	52
	1-5-1	Development of Special Needs Education System	65
	5-1	The Competent Authorities	112

Table	8-1	Relation between General and Educational Administration	143
	8-2	Education Committee Occupation	154
	9-1	Status of the Amount of a Purpose-oriented Expenditure	162
	9-2	Breakdown of Educational Expenses by Type	163
	9-3	Breakdown of Educational Expenses by Purpose	164
	11-1	Compulsory Education Schools	189
Pic.	1-1-1	Making Soil for Planting Rice Seeds (5 years old)	24
	1-1-2	Happy Time with Senior Supporters	31
	1-4-1	One Scene of National Center Test for University Admission	57
	3-1	Staff Meeting	87
	4-1	In-service Training for New Principals	104
	4-2	Lesson Study	107
	6-1	Mobile Library	119
	6-2	One of the Activities of a Community Learning Center (Tea Ceremony)	120
	12-1	The First Secondary School	196

Introduction: Background of Present Japanese Educational System

1. Modernized Japanese Education from the Second half of 19th Century

In 1872 a new educational system was introduced by the central government and from that time, education quickly became widely accepted throughout the country. This trend depended on the past era's situation in which people were likely to accept basic education as useful and very much essential for their daily life which stemmed from the new central government's policy to make Japan stronger and wealthier. It was essential to educate people with modern knowledge and skills to realize this policy. In this context, the government adopted a policy to employ a certain number of western people who were experts in each field, started to investigate the developed educational systems of advanced countries, and also decided to send students abroad for their studies.

The government prepared a gradual educational system effectively from primary to higher education. It is surprising that the rate of enrolment in four years compulsory education reached more than 90% by the end of 19th century and after that it continued to increase steadily. Such expansion had been promoted by the development of industries and subsequent improvements in the standard of living.

Although Japanese people used to respect knowledge and cultural activities, steady development of education in a short time owed to the firm policy of the new government. In this system, the central government directed the local authorities to develop it and each school was expected to perform the role planned by the central government. This system was used effectively to defuse education nationwide quickly, but it faulted by not accepting local needs and peculiarities.

Thus, education in Japan during that period developed year by year, but it was irreparably damaged because of the defeat of World War II. Japan had to face her reconstruction into a country seeking peace and democracy.

2. After World War II

After being defeated in World War II, Japan started with a new Constitution in which the value of peace and democracy was clearly declared. At the same time, people's fundamental human rights were provided in it as well. All persons had the right to an education and such provision expanded the opportunity for education. The system was reorganized very simply from preschool to the university level. Being under the occupation by Allied Forces, mainly of the United States, it was quite natural that the new policy was affected by the United States. However, some policies were succeeded from the former system.

The new educational system changed who had authority. The power belonged to local authorities, not to the central government, because education is very much close to the people and also, educational policy should depend on the public opinion of the area. The newly introduced education committee was composed of local area representatives. Under the previous system, information as to the nation-wide education system was regularly provided by the central government. However, its role was reduced under the new system.

However, this new idea faded out gradually for several reasons. The shortage of local finances, lack of experience to maintain it, a lasting opinion to have uniform education of all over the country, serious confrontation in politics regarding how to secure education effectively and neutrally and so on all contributed to the gradual transfer of power over education back to the central government.

As the economic reconstruction after the War had been realized very quickly in particular from the 1960's, there was a high demand for man-power in all industries. Also this steady progress brought about better living standards and people were able to afford to pay for their child's education. This economic growth arose from the philosophy of the peace-loving Post-war Constitution which freed people from the burden of military expenses. Thus, the flourishing economy brought an opportunity to expand education and people could enjoy attending school and other institutions after compulsory education. This trend can be recognized in **Fig.1-1** below.

Fig.1-1 Percentage of Students for Post -compulsory Education

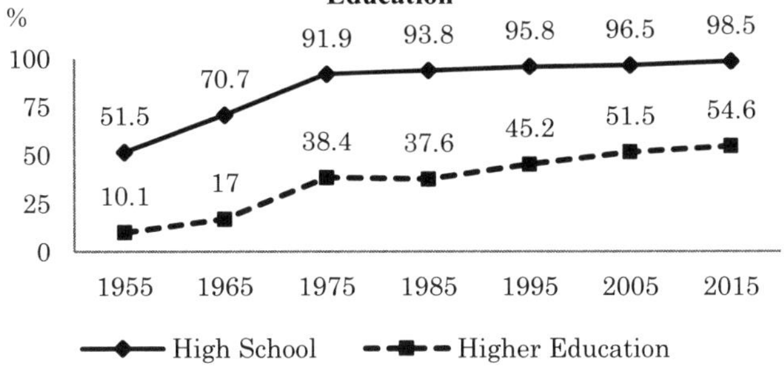

%
100
75
50
25
0

51.5   70.7   91.9   93.8   95.8   96.5   98.5

10.1   17   38.4   37.6   45.2   51.5   54.6

1955   1965   1975   1985   1995   2005   2015

High School   Higher Education

(MEXT, Report on School Basic Survey: each year)

However this educational expansion involves a lot of problems. Firstly, the extension of the period of education could be desirable to increase intelligence among people as a whole, but it is doubtful that a wide range of knowledge would necessarily be accepted by them. They are likely to think that school is an effective tool to get better employment. Secondly, as people think that it is natural for all youngsters to attend schools as long as possible, not going could be viewed as failure which makes declining to pursue a higher education even more difficult. Youngsters are obliged to be students of any school without any clear direction to improve their growth. Such problem should be resolved as soon as possible.

3. Problems of Recent Years

Education is very much important for everybody, and it can play a social role at the same time. From this point of view, it could be recognized that social trends could affect education. We are going to show how what is going on in society affects present day education.

(1) Academic achievement

So many children go to school and are given opportunities to improve themselves. Parents are likely to be interested in their achievements and also people observe their performance at school. It is natural that children can actively enjoy their school life and are asked to develop their abilities, not only knowledge but a lot of skills. In this context the quality of school education has been one of the targets of argument so far. The beginning of such anxiety was the result of PISA (Programme for International Students Assessment) of OECD (Organization for Economic and Cultural Development) in 2003 which showed the standard of Japanese education had declined. The Japanese Central Government recognized the precise research and from 2007 nationwide examinations have been regularly carried out. Improved academic achievement of children is naturally demanded, but they are also asked to have a sound relation with others and to develop their ability to communicate. At present, such multi-faceted programs should be developed for Japanese education.

(2) Declining birth rate

Japan has faced a lot of gradual changes in society, in particular the decreasing birth rate over the past forty years. **(Fig.1-2)** It is said that the rate of women in the workforce in Japan has increased up to the present days and the number of nuclear families have grown, especially in urban areas. However, the number of facilities to support child rearing have not been provided effectively according to this trend. Also people are likely to prefer a few numbers of children because such circumstances would be favorable for children as well as parents.

Fig.1-2 Number of Newborn Babies (ten thousand)

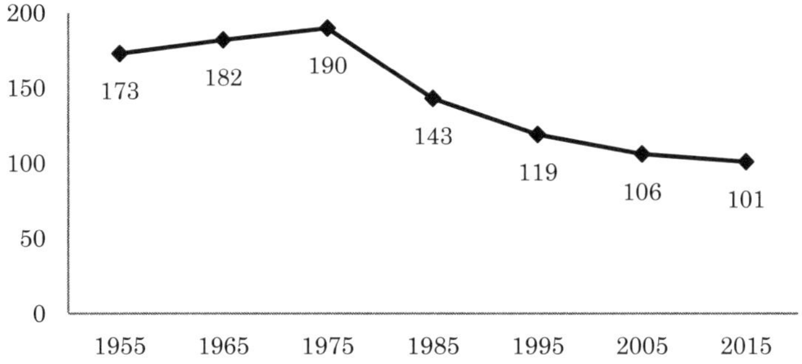

173　182　190　143　119　106　101

1955　1965　1975　1985　1995　2005　2015

(Ministry of Health, Labor & Welfare, Demographic Statistics, 2015)

Consequently, the population in Japan is projected to decrease in the near future. Such a state will bring about a labor shortage which may affect the industrial structure, economic growth, and so on.

At the same time, this declining birth rate has an effect on education. For example smaller school and class sizes, school consolidation or integration, and decreasing numbers of school teachers. Furthermore, it became urgent to consider the number of places for students in upper secondary schools and higher education institutions.

(3) Disparity in economic standard of family

Every family expects their children's sound growing and parents are likely to sufficiently promote their education. On the other hand society has realized that education is quite important for them and for its future. From this context, it is quite valuable that the Constitution describes the right to an education for all people and free compulsory education.

However, this constitutional provision is interpreted as just tuition and textbook costs, not all compulsory school expenses. It means parents have to pay for school meals, supplies, extra-curricular activities, school excursions and so on. Additionally, parents who hope their children will do well in school, tend to attend out of school activities including "Juku", when they can afford to pay.

It has become quite natural to go to upper secondary, which is not compulsory in Japan, and parents must pay all its expenses and if they expect their child to continue their education afterward, their financial burdens become heavier. On the contrary, in the case of a family whose living standard is below average, their children may have to be discouraged from pursuing higher levels of education because of the increased financial burden it would place on the family.

The declining birth rate was indicated in the previous section and this situation could be understood as a reflection of such economic burdens placed on families.

It is also worth pointing out that the disparity in household income has increased according to the stagnation of Japanese economy and employment. This situation has affected the length and quality of the education of children. In another words, the principle of an equal opportunity for education has been distorted gradually. It is recognized that education levels correlate to one's living standards. Year by year, the number of families which belong to lower economic conditions has increased. This positively correlates with the increased number of children seeking educational support from their local governments (**Fig.1-3**). Such a serious problem should be resolved in cooperation with the department of welfare.

(4) Internationalization

Generally, modern society was based on state, but the range of its activities has expanded from local to world-wide. At present, manufacturing and consumption are not solely performed in one country but are dependent on the international market. It means that one country cannot be economically independent and must be involved in the global economy.

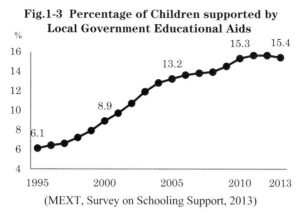

Fig.1-3 Percentage of Children supported by Local Government Educational Aids

(MEXT, Survey on Schooling Support, 2013)

This progress includes active trade and consequently promotes human mobility. The number of people who come and go across national borders has steadily increased and some have moved to find new jobs, education, or opportunities in other countries. Such a situation has been accelerated by wars, disasters, starvation, poverty, and other traumatic events. Additionally this active movement promotes mutual understanding and enhances opportunities to smoothly exchange useful information. This could be thought of as one reason for the recent rapid development of Information and Communication Technology (ICT).

Japan cannot stand on the sidelines of this situation. On the contrary Japan is expected to play a certain role in realizing international prosperity and peace. For example, to understand current global issues, improvement of personal communication skills should be taught in schools and able persons should be trained in all fields for possible technological cooperation and humanitarian support.

Part 1

Schools and Educational System

Chapter 1. Schools

§1. Early Childhood Education and Care

1. Large Scale Reform of Early Childhood Education and Care (ECEC) System

In August 2012, the Act on Child and Childcare Support and related laws were passed, and from April 2015, the "Comprehensive Support System for Children and Child-Rearing ("The New System" in this chapter) aimed at drastic expansion and improvement of the child-rearing support system started. Behind this reform, there lies the problem of waiting children for ECEC facilities.

Pic.1-1-1 Making Soil for Planting Rice Seeds (5 years old)

(Dietary Promotion Act requires all ECEC facilities to provide dietary education.)

The Japanese Constitution states that Japanese citizens have a right to education, and the Child Welfare Law guarantees that all children have equal rights to all welfare services. However, in reality, the public system is not catching up with the growing needs due to the rising educational background of women, international pressures, and the policy for gender equality in society.

Around 1996, dual-income families increased drastically [1] and in 1999 the number of children attending nursery centers surpassed those attending kindergarten. In 2015, almost 100 % of children above 4 years of age attended some form of center based ECEC facilities: 48% at kindergarten, about 50% at nursery centers. The number of kindergartens also decreased. All early ECEC facilities including kindergartens, are trying to meet the growing demands for childcare.

2. Integration of Early Childhood Education and Care [2]

One of the innovations under the New System was to reorganize the dual system governed by the MEXT and the Ministry of Health, Labor and Welfare (MHLW) into a single system. It is the integration of education with welfare. To be more precise, it is to integrate kindergartens which are "schools" based on the School Education Law (SEL), and the nursery centers which are "child welfare institutions" based on the Child Welfare Law into one single facility to provide comprehensive child-rearing support under the same government office. Both the financial system and educational content were made common. The Center for ECEC, 'Nintei Kodomo En' (authorized children's center) was launched in 2006, but they were still governed by two Ministries. There were four types of Centers for ECEC (ECEC Center in this paper): Kindergarten-Nursery Center Collaborative type (K-N Collaborative type), Kindergarten Based type, Nursery Center Based type and Local Discretion type. Under the New System, K-N type was reborn with a new legal identity, and is administered by the Cabinet Office.

---

1 Cabinet Office, '*White Paper on Gender Equality* (in Japanese)', 2016, p.47.

2 Masaaki Okada (1970), *Japanese System of Early Childhood Education and Care*, Froebelkan (in Japanese). Tsumori, Kubo, Honda (1959), *History of Kindergarten*, Kouseisha Kouseikaku (in Japanese).

3. Open to All Children based on Child Care Certification

Under the New System, all children who need childcare must receive Child Care Certification at the municipal office. Certification ranges from 1 to 3 according to the degree of needs (**Table 1-1-1**). The contract is made between parents and ECEC institutions based on the type of certification.

Table 1-1-1 Categories of ECEC Certification under the New System

Certification	Criteria	Hours Served	Facilities Accessible
Type 1	Over 3 years old No child care	Education standard hours (4 hours)	Kindergarten Center for ECEC
Type 2	Over 3 years old Need child care	ECEC short hours (8hrs) ECEC standard hours (11hrs)	Center for ECEC Nursery center
Type 3	Under 3 years old Need child care	ECEC short hours (8hrs) ECEC standard hours (11hrs)	Center for ECEC Nursery center Local Child Care Services

4. Diversified Facilities of ECEC

The New System provides a variety of ECEC facilities to meet the growing needs. In addition to center based facilities, such as kindergartens, nursery centers, ECEC centers, small sized EC services for under 2 years old, and private company funded ECEC services were institutionalized (**Fig. 1-1-1**).

Fig. 1-1-1 ECEC Facilities in Japan (July 2017)

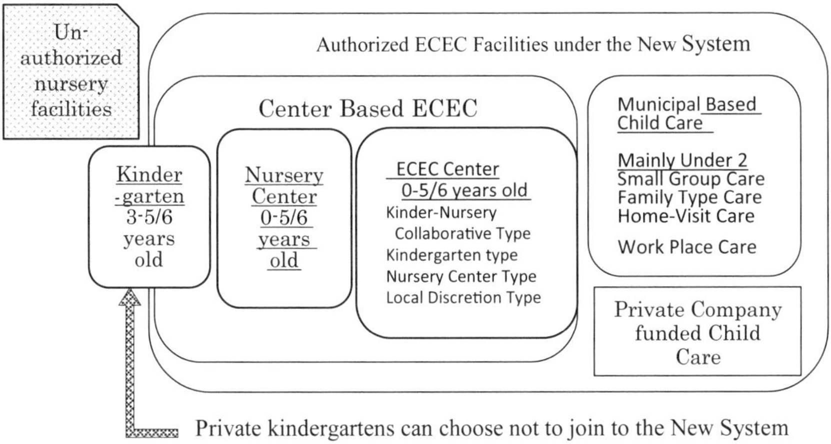

Un-authorized nursery facilities

Authorized ECEC Facilities under the New System

Center Based ECEC

Municipal Based Child Care

Kinder-garten 3-5/6 years old

Nursery Center 0-5/6 years old

ECEC Center 0-5/6 years old
Kinder-Nursery Collaborative Type
Kindergarten type
Nursery Center Type
Local Discretion Type

Mainly Under 2
Small Group Care
Family Type Care
Home-Visit Care

Work Place Care

Private Company funded Child Care

Private kindergartens can choose not to join to the New System

(Source: prepared by author)

1) Kindergarten

The purpose and goals of kindergarten is prescribed in the School Education Law (SEL). Kindergarten is regarded as the stage to form the basis of life-long character formation. As the beginning of school, kindergarten promotes the development of mind and body by providing an appropriate environment. Kindergarten education is provided based on the national curriculum framework for kindergarten set by the Minister of MEXT. In 2008, the related law was revised so that children from the age of 2 years old can be accepted as a part of child- rearing support. Standard education hours are 4 hours per day. Education weeks should not be less than 39 weeks per year. With the increase of ECEC needs, kindergarten also started to take care of children after regular education hours. Almost 100 % of private kindergartens are taking care of children after regular hours, some as late as 7 p.m. In 2016, about 63% of kindergartens were private institutions. Private kindergartens have 3 choices: to stay in the old system, join the New System as a kindergarten, or convert to an ECEC center in the New System.

2) Nursery Center

The purpose of the nursery center is to provide care and education for children of certification 2 and 3. The ranges from 0 to 5/6 years old as described above (Table 1-1-1). Standard ECEC hours are 11 hours, and short ECEC hours are 8 hours. Opening hours is basically 8 hours, but considering the condition of the community, the head of the nursery center can decide the working hours. Generally, there are 300 working days per year. Extended hours can exceed 11 hours par day and in general, working hours are increasing.

The content of education and care is based on the "Nursery center Guidelines" set by the Minister of MHLW. The teachers are required to hold the nursery teachers qualification. However, like kindergarten, more and more teachers are expected to hold teacher credentials as well.

3) Center for ECEC

A Center for ECEC is an authorized children's center which serves all children with Type 1, 2, or 3 certifications (from 0 to 5/6 years old). It has the comprehensive function of a nursery center, kindergarten, and child-rearing support for parents with small children who live in the community it serves. The advantage of both kindergarten and nursery center was combined to create an ECEC Center. For children over 3 years old and do not need care, standard education hours are 4 hours as in kindergarten. Education weeks for whole year must be over 39 weeks. For under 2 years old children with the Type 3 or 3 certification, hours of education and care is decided by the head of each school with a basic principle of 8 hours (it can be opened up to 11 hours a day) as a nursery center.

In the curriculum framework, the consistency between nursery centers for children under 2 years old, kindergartens for children over 3 years old, and the alignment with primary school education are secured. Also, the smooth transition to primary school is emphasized. ECEC teachers are expected to hold a nursery teacher qualification and a teachers' credential for kindergarten. At K-N type ECEC Centers under the New System, above all, teachers are called "hoiku-kyoyu" (ECEC teacher), and are required to hold both qualifications. The government is encouraging all teachers working at ECEC facilities to hold both qualifications.

5. Innovation of Content and Method of ECEC

There are 3 national curriculum frameworks for content and method, for kindergartens, nursery centers, and K-N Centers for ECEC. They are revised every ten years. The curriculum framework for K-N type ECEC Centers was made public first time in 2015. The revised frameworks for kindergartens and nursery centers were made public in March 2017. Major innovations are:

(1) educational content over 3 years old are made common in all three curriculum frameworks,

(2) the consistency and alignment of content and curriculum management within primary schools is secured,

(3) educational function at nursery centers is clearly stated, and education and care is to be provided comprehensively at both nursery centers and Centers for ECEC, and

(4) the "Desirable Growth by the End of Early Childhood" is set to be shared among all ECEC facilities (see **Table 1-1-2**).

Table 1-1-2 Desirable Growth by the End of Early Childhood

(1) Healthy mind and body	(2) Independent mind	(3) Cooperative attitude
(4) Emerging sense of moral and norms	(5) Social attitude	(6) Emerging ability to think
(7) Connection to nature and respect of life		
(8) Interest in numbers, quantities, shapes, signs, letters		
(9) Communicating with words	(10) Rich sensibility and expression	

Early childhood education in Japan is basically holistic. The content is categorized into 5 areas (health, human relationship, environment, words, and expression), but the learning and teaching of all these areas must be done comprehensively through the environment and play. Throughout early childhood education, children's independence, the life and environment suitable for childhood and for mental/physical development are the main focus. Early childhood education is not regarded as preparatory education for primary school. However, three pillars that penetrate education through primary school were made clear by the revision of the curriculum framework. They are: (1) knowledge and skill, (2) cognitive, expression and thinking skills, and (3) attitude towards learning and humanity. It is important that children have a fulfilling time and experiences suitable for this particular stage. Teachers organize the creative environment where a variety of plays spring up and are developed by children themselves so that they acquire desirable characters and competencies by the end of early childhood.

6. Heading towards Free ECEC

Under the New System, fees for all ECEC facilities are decided mainly according to the financial abilities of parents based on National Standards. The government is taking steps to eliminate all ECEC fees. At present, regardless of the type of facility, the second child is half the price and the third child is free.

7. Challenges

Public expectation for the New System was larger than opportunity created by the New System. The number of children who exceeded the available spaces, and teachers are in short supply. There are a large number of unauthorized child-care facilities which creates public concern for the quality of education and care. In addition, under the New System, rapid privatization of ECEC facilities is making headway. The new type of governing body, "public-private coalition legal entity," was created and a new type of governance never experienced before is in progress. At the same time however, public facilities are drastically decreasing. It is not sure what will be the long term effects of growing privatization in ECEC.

Pic. 1-1-2 Happy Time with Senior Supporters

(Fundamental Law of Education prescribes the promotion of collaboration between schools, homes, and community to share the responsibility for children's education with whole community)

§2. Primary Education

1. Outline of Primary Education
(1) Principle, Purpose, Length of Education and Providers of Primary School

The principle of primary education in Japan is compulsory, free and neutral. In terms of compulsory education, it is fixed by the Constitution of Japan and Fundamental Law of Education (FLE) that citizens shall be obligated to have children under their protection receive a general education and the central and local governments shall be responsible for the implementation of compulsory education in order to guarantee the opportunity for compulsory education and its adequate standards. As for free education, no tuition fee shall be charged in schools provided by the central and local governments. Neutrality is required for political and religious education. Political neutrality means that schools are strictly prohibited from undertaking political propaganda or political activities for or against any specific political party. On the other hand, religious neutrality means that public schools must refrain from religious instruction or activities of a specific religion.

According to article 29 of the School Education Law (SEL), the purpose of primary school is to give children basic education of ordinary topics conducted as compulsory education depending on their physical and mental development. In order to achieve this purpose, acquisition of basic knowledge and skills, cultivation of the ability to think, judge, and express something with said knowledge and skills, and fostering behavior to actively learn are emphasized.

Parents and guardians should make their children receive nine years of compulsory education altogether. They are asked to enroll their children in primary schools from the beginning of the fiscal year after their sixth birthday to the end of the fiscal year which includes their twelfth birthday. Primary school consists of six grade and students are promoted to the next grade according to their age, but there are quite few who must repeat a year.

However, some people insist that a six-year primary school is not suitable for present day. In this context, a new type of 'compulsory education school ', which provides nine years of compulsory education from primary school to lower secondary school launched in 2016.

Municipalities have a duty to provide primary school in their areas[3]. In addition, state and Incorporated Education Institutions (IEI) can also do it as well (state and private school). There are about 20,000 primary schools in Japan and most of them are maintained by municipalities, and as a result, almost of all students belong to them at present.

(2) School Attendance Zone and Choice of School

A municipality's board of education is required to prepare student's school registration they will attend. In fact, they must make a list of six-year old students and the school they will enter. When there are more than two primary schools in the municipality, they must designate a primary school each student belongs to. Many municipalities have school attendance zones in their territory and designate schools according to them. However, if parents request, students are allowed to attend other schools if there are some reasons such as the child's physical condition and bullying.

Moreover, there are some municipalities where parents can choose their child's school that are apart from the designated authorized schools. According to research by MEXT, in 2012 out of 1,753 municipal boards of education, 1,547 boards of education (88.2%) provided more than two primary schools in their areas, of which 246 municipalities (15.9%) introduced the school choice system. There are many ways parents can choose. Some cases are shown below. Firstly, students are allowed to go to any school they want in the municipality's area. Secondly, they can choose one among a few schools the education committee designates in advance, and thirdly, leaving the traditional system, an

---

3 Special wards (There are 23 special wards in Tokyo only) can establish primary schools.

exceptional school designated by the board of education can enroll students from any area within its municipality.

2. Present Situation of Primary Schools
(1) School year and term

The school year begins in April and ends in March of the following year. 80% of schools divide the school year into three terms: the first term is from April to July, the second is from September to December, and the third is from January to March. There are long breaks between the terms: about a 40-day summer holiday, two-week winter holiday and spring holiday. The length of a school term is decided by local authorities in order to secure the required number of class hours, some schools introduce a two-term system.

Since the 2002 school year, the five-day week system has been fully introduced in Japan; schools are closed on Saturdays in addition to Sundays. It was aimed at cultivating a 'zest for living', which includes students' abilities to learn and think by themselves, and life enrichment by giving them a lot of opportunities for experiential activities through cooperation between schools, families and local communities. On the other hand, it has been pointed out that quite a few students do not necessarily spend their time meaningfully. To securing the required number of school hours, MEXT revised a part of the regulation to allow boards of education to have Saturday classes at their own discretion in 2013.

(2) Classes

Students of the same age study together in classrooms. Class size in primary schools should be less than 40 students, limited to 35 students during their first year. Though the standard for class size is defined by the central government, each prefecture can define its own standard, which can be less than the central government's standard. Considering these points, local authorities have flexibility in setting the class size standard based on school-specific and local circumstances. The average class size is 23.9 students; the student-teacher rate is 15.5:1. The class size and the student-teacher rate have been decreasing from year to year.

Classes in primary schools function not only as learning groups, where learning activities such as learning a subject are conducted, but also as a life experience group that creates basic life circumstances and desirable human relationships to perform during school life. A classroom teacher is responsible for class management and can teach any subject, however, classes led by subject-specific teachers have been increasing recently. As the grade goes up, assigning a subject-specific teacher is often implemented. The percentage of cases when schools have teachers in charge of a specific subject is 48.9% for science, 60.2% for music, 22.9% for art and handcrafts, and 36.5% for home economics. In addition, small group lessons such as ability-grouped lessons and team teaching sessions are organized. Individualized instructions are also developing.

3. Curriculum
(1) The Course of Study

Article 33 of the SEL provides that the MEXT prescribes the curriculum for primary schools, and its specific contents are fixed by the Ordinance for Enforcement of SEL. The course of study defines the detailed standard of the curriculum. The regulation has been partly changed and school education based on the newly revised central standard curriculum will start in 2020. This consists of various subjects, moral education as a special subject, foreign language activities, a period for integrated studies, and special activities. The subjects include Japanese language, social studies, arithmetic, science, living environment studies, music, art and handicraft, home economics, physical education, and foreign language. The living environment studies is provided only for first and second grade students, whereas third grade and above students study social studies and science. Under the current curriculum, Japanese students begin to learn foreign language as a subject from the first grade of lower secondary school, but it has been changed to start from the fifth grade of primary school. As a result, reading and writing skills will start to be taught at the primary school level. Foreign language activities, mainly in listening and speaking, aim to familiarize students to a foreign language (before formally studying it as a subject). Its target was changed from the fifth and sixth grade students to third and fourth grade students.

Table 1-2-1 Numbers of Each Subject in a Year (Primary School, 2020-)

Category		1st	2nd	3rd	4th	5th	6th
Subject	Japanese Language	306	315	245	245	175	175
	Social Studies	-	-	70	90	100	105
	Arithmetic	136	175	175	175	175	175
	Science	-	-	90	105	105	105
	Living Environment Studies	102	105	-	-	-	-
	Music	68	70	60	60	50	50
	Art and Handicraft	68	70	60	60	50	50
	Home Economics	-	-	-	-	60	55
	Physical Education	102	105	105	105	90	90
	Foreign Language	-	-	-	-	70	70
Moral Education as a Special Subject		34	35	35	35	35	35
Foreign Language Activities		-	-	35	35	-	-
Period for Integrated Studies		-	-	70	70	70	70
Special Activities		34	35	35	35	35	35
Total		850	910	980	1015	1015	1015

(MEXT, publicly announced in March 2017)

In primary schools, one day consists of 6, 45-minute periods of study. The minimum number of weeks in a primary school year is 35 weeks (34 weeks for first grade students). On average, actual classes are given for more than 40 weeks. The standard hours of class session in primary schools under the Ordinance for Enforcement of the SEL are as described in Table 1-2-1. 70% of schools exceed the indicated standard hours. Although the timetable has been overcrowded until now, the number of class hours further increased due to the new course of study. It is pointed out that it is necessary to learn quickly in units of 45 minutes and to have a resilient time schedule, and make use of long holidays or Saturdays, etc., according to the circumstances of each school and area.

(2) The Debate on declining academic performance and curriculum

In 2002, the five-day school week system was launched and the course of study was revised and fully implemented. The learning contents were carefully selected and 'the period for integrated study' was introduced in order to foster each child's 'zest for living'. However, in spite of the fact that reading comprehension ranked higher in the Programme for International Student Assessment (PISA) 2000, it ranked as low as 8th among 28 countries, and 'declining academic achievement' became a social problem. In response to this, the MEXT launched the idea of 'certain academic achievement' in 1998, but the course of study which aimed at realizing relaxed educational activities became the target of criticism, and led to its partial revision in 2003 after its full implementation. However, even in PISA 2003, the reading comprehension ranking continued to drop, ranked as low as 12th among 30 countries and 'relaxed education' was reviewed, resulting in the increase in class hours. With regard to nurturing the 'zest for living', while emphasizing its importance as before, teaching came to aim at nurturing academic skills, consisting of the acquisition of well-balanced knowledge, virtue and health, one that is neither 'relaxed' nor 'jam-packed'.

The National Assessment of Academic Ability was conducted starting in 2007 and efforts to improve academic achievement were implemented in various regions. The results led to reading comprehension ranking first among 34 countries in PISA 2012. Even though reading comprehension ranked sixth in 35 countries in PISA 2015, it can be said that the depreciation of academic achievement has stopped and that things are picking up for the better. Although it can be said that overall academic ability has improved in this way, the elimination of academic discrepancies remains a challenge even now.

4. Special Activity

Special activity is one of the characteristic curriculums of Japan. The contents of special activities are class activities, student's council activities, club activities, and school events. School events include ceremonial events (entrance ceremony, graduation ceremony, opening and closing ceremony of the school term etc.), cultural events (school arts festival, exhibition of student's works, music concert, etc.), health and safety/physical education events (medical examination, athletic games, disaster drill, etc.), excursions/group lodging events (school excursion, school trip, outdoor activities, etc.), and labor productivity/volunteering events (plant cultivation and animal breeding activities, cleaning activities in the local area, and interacting with welfare facilities). Special activities are carried out throughout the school year with large groups, formed for the entire school or for the school year. They aim at the formation of desirable human relationships, deepening the sense of affiliation and solidarity of the group, cultivation of public spirit and cooperation to build a better life. While aiming to nurture practical attitudes, they bring a needed order and change to school life. In addition, special activities are carried out, not only in primary schools, but also in lower and upper secondary schools. Those activities are conducted according to the developmental stages of the children.

5. Current Problems

Changes in today's society influence children in different ways. In this section, the popularization of the Internet and child poverty which influence children and young people including primary school students are explained. Both problems are serious because the careless use of the Internet can lead to bullying and child poverty can influence their future.

(1) Popularization of the Internet

With the popularization of the Internet, the number of children who enjoy their leisure time using the Internet has increased. According to research conducted by the Cabinet Office, 61.3 % of primary school students answered that they use the Internet with some Internet accessible devices such as smartphones. What children do on the Internet depends on the kind of device they use. For example, primary school students using smartphones play games (72.9%), see motion pictures (53.5%), communicate (43.9%), search information (42.6%), and so on[4].

As children's use of the Internet has become popular, some problems have occurred. For example, some children meet strangers on the Internet and get involved in affairs or crimes, or some children abuse or bully other children on the Internet. Therefore, education on how to use the Internet properly and safely is required.

Also, using Information and Communication Technology (ICT) in classes has been required. In order to increase the interest and the desire to learn or promote learning based on each child's ability and features, equipment, such as electronic blackboards and tablets have been introduced.

(2) Children's poverty

With the increase in the number of irregularly employed and single-parent families, child poverty has become a serious problem. According to the Central Livelihood Survey conducted by the Ministry of Health, Labor and Welfare (2013), the percentage of children under 17 living in poverty is 16.3 %.

Child poverty influences children's health. For instance, the survey conducted by Adachi Ward, Tokyo in 2015 shows that 19.7 % of disadvantaged children have more than five bad teeth, higher than that of non-disadvantaged children

---

4   Cabinet Office, *'The Research Report on the Actual Condition of the Environment for Youth's Internet Use* (in Japanese)', 2016, pp.20, 48

(10.1%)[5].

Moreover, it has become apparent that child poverty also influences children's motivation and academic achievement. In research conducted in 2012 in Osaka City on fifth grade primary school students and second grade public lower secondary students and their parents, 12% of primary school students and 14% of lower secondary school students were living in poverty. Compared to children who were not living in poverty, a larger percentage of children in poverty answered 'disagree' to the questions such as 'If I try hard, I will get rewarded', 'I am a person of value', and 'I look forward to my future'. This shows that children in poverty tend to have low self-efficacy and there is incentive disparity[6]. Also, 'The research study concerning the analysis of the factor on academic achievement based on the result of nationwide surveys on academic ability and learning situation (detailed research)' shows that household socioeconomic backgrounds affect children's academic achievement. For instance, children with affluent socioeconomic backgrounds (indicator based on household income, father and mother's academic background) tend to have a higher percentage of questions answered correctly in each subject and question[7]. This shows that children in poverty have a relative disadvantage.

As just described, child poverty is the serious problem which influences children's growth, for example, child poverty leads to a disparity in health and academic achievement. In 2014, a law concerning enhancing the measure for child poverty came into force so that the circumstances where children living in poverty can grow soundly are made and equal opportunity in education can be completed instead of children's future depending on the circumstances in which

---

5   Adachi Ward, Tokyo '*The Report on the Actual Condition of the Children's Health and Life in 2015* (in Japanese)', p.32

6   Takafumi Uzuhashi, Aya Abe, Hirotoshi Yano, '*The Research on Children in Osaka : Brief Summary of the Result* (in Japanese)', 2014, pp.16,29,31-32

7   Ochanomizu University, '*The Research Study concerning the Analysis of the Factor on Academic Achievement based on the Result of Nationwide Surveys on Academic Ability and Learning Situation (detailed research)* (in Japanese)', 2014, p.7

they grow. With this law, support for education, support for life, job assistance and economic support for parents are provided.

Column-1: One day in Primary School

The starting time of primary school is around 8:00 a.m. Teachers arrive at a school before the time students arrive at and prepare for the day's lesson. On hearing bell rings, homeroom teachers and students have a morning meeting in each classroom. The teacher tells the students the day's schedule and grasps their physical condition. Then, the majority of primary schools set a short learning time named "Morning Activities". Students do various activities assigned to the day of the week, for example reading, review exercises of arithmetic, and so on.

Table 1-2-2
One day in Primary School

8:10	Open
Morning Meeting (10min)	
Morning Activities (20min)	
8:50 ~ 9:35	1st period
Recess (10min)	
9:45 ~ 10:30	2nd period
Recess (15min)	
10:45 ~ 11:30	3rd period
Recess (10min)	
11:40 ~ 12:25	4th period
School Lunch (50min)	
Noon Recess (30min)	
Cleaning (15min)	
14:00 ~ 14:45	5th period
Recess (10min)	
14:55 ~ 15:40	6th period
End-of-Day Meeting (20min)	
Supplementary Class (20min)	
16:40	Close

One class is 45 minutes. Students have four classes in the morning and one or two classes in the afternoon. Many classes are taught by a homeroom teacher but classes for some special subjects, for example music, home economics, and drawing and crafts are often taught by other teachers with a license for that special subject. There is a recess for 10~15 minutes between each class. After morning classes, there is time for lunch, a noon recess, and cleaning. The job of serving food to each student and cleaning up after is assigned in turn to groups composed of about 10 students. All students take part in cleaning the schoolhouse and facilities. After the last class in the afternoon, homeroom teachers and students have the end-of-day meeting in each classroom. Students review the day and will have their own goal for tomorrow. Students leave school at around 3:00 p.m. when they have five classes and at around 4:00 p.m. when they have six classes.

Staff meetings and in-school teacher training are held once a week. Teachers also respond to the demands from parents or community residents regarding school matters. Closing time is around 5:00 p.m. but many teachers work overtime.

Chapter 1. Schools 43

§3. Secondary Education

1. Summary of the Current System (Lower Secondary Schools)
(1) General purpose of lower secondary school

The purpose of lower secondary schools as prescribed is to provide general education conducted as compulsory education in accordance with the physical and mental development of students based on the education they received at primary schools. (School Education Law: SEL)

As for enrollment, parents are to "ensure their children receive education at lower secondary schools for 3 years from 12 to 15 years old (including lower secondary schools for special needs education schools).

In addition, municipalities are required to establish enough schools so that the compulsory education requirement is fulfilled. However that could be established by not only municipalities but also the central government, local public bodies and Incorporated Educational Institutions (IEI). For establishing lower secondary schools, minimum standards are stipulated for classroom size, area of school buildings, grounds and required facilities etc.

In this system, the central government makes a brief guideline firstly as a national standard. Local governments can decide their standards according to local circumstances. Also each municipal board of education is allowed to organize actual class size individually.

The standards for class formation provide the maximum number of students per class, 40 in the case of lower secondary schools. On the contrary two classes of different grades can be combined into one class in rural areas and flexible organization of classes such as small-group teaching and team teaching can be approved if necessary.

Compulsory Schools including lower secondary schools are provided for students who live relatively near to the school and such an attendance zone is decided by the municipalities basically according to the capacity of school. However, such regulation was recently revised. Firstly when the designated school is not fit for the student, the education committee can recognize a change depending on the parents' appeal, and secondly, parental choice is accepted if there is more than one school nearby.

(2) Curriculum

Curriculum is a plan to achieve the purpose of school and is prepared to fit local and individual circumstances. As for lower secondary schools, the principal as the head of the school is responsible for curriculum development just like primary schools. The current course of study is to be revised in 2017 and is scheduled to be fully implemented in 2021.

The proposed new revisions require further improvement from the perspective of "active and interactive deep learning" or so-called active learning and the enhancement of programming education in the fields of Industrial Arts and Homemaking. In addition, further consideration is required regarding a sustainable approach for extra-curricular club activities in the future by taking into consideration the accelerated decline in birth rate, as well as a reduction of the burden placed on teaching staff.

Table 1-3-1 Numbers of Each Subject in Lower Secondary School (2008)

	Category	1st	2nd	3rd
	Japanese Language	140	140	105
	Social Studies	105	105	140
	Mathematics	140	105	140
	Science	105	140	140
Subject	Music	45	35	35
	Art	45	35	35
	Health and Physical Education	105	105	105
	Industrial Arts and Home Making	70	70	35
	Foreign Language	140	140	140
Moral Education		35	35	35
Comprehensive Learning		50	70	70
Special Activities		35	35	35
Total		1015	1015	1015

Lesson hours stated in this table, 1 credit hour is 50 minutes of instruction. (Lower Secondary school Curriculum Guidelines as of March 2008)

(3) Issues in lower secondary schools

Lower secondary school education currently faces a wide range of various issues, one of which is "difficulties faced by first-grade students". In other words, it is a problem when such students become physically and mentally unstable due to differences between primary and lower secondary school education. The figure below indicates mental instability. According to the results of a survey conducted by the Japan Society of School Health Education, lower secondary school students who answered that "they feel "frequently" or "sometimes" like doing nothing because they are depressed" account for almost 40% for male students and almost 50% for female students. The results also show that nearly 40% of students answered that they had problems concentrating.

Fig. 1-3-1 Mental Health of Students (%)

		Frequently	Sometimes	occasionally	Not at all
I feel like doing nothing due to depression.	boy	17.6	19.4	31.2	31.8
	girl	25.5	23	31.1	20.4
I cannot concentrate and think quickly.	boy	17.5	21.5	34.6	26.4
	girl	18.1	24.7	37.4	19.8

☐ Frequently (about once a week)　　☐ Sometimes (about once a month)
☒ occasionally (less than once a month)　☐ Not at all

(Japan Society of School Health, *Students and Students Health Condition Surveillance Report*, 2012)

There are also problems regarding their study habits. According to the results of a survey conducted by the MEXT of 2016, about 30% of students studied less than one hour on weekdays (Monday to Friday) outside of their schools, and 50% on weekends.

In order to respond to these issues, individual-oriented teaching is required at schools to enhance students' motivation. Its survey shows that 96.4% of lower secondary schools are likely to adopt various policies to improve this situation, mainly by team teaching.

Whatever the learning unit could be, such a system is likely to depend on the achievement level of students, not on their interests. Individual-oriented teaching based on student interests presents an opportunity to introduce active learning.

Fig. 1-3-2 Situation of Individual-based Teaching (%)

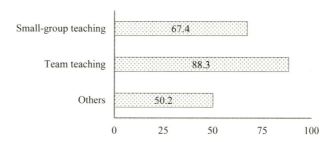

(MEXT, *2015 Survey on the Situation of the Development and Implementation of Curriculums*)

Fig. 1-3-3 Situation of Individual-based Learning (%)

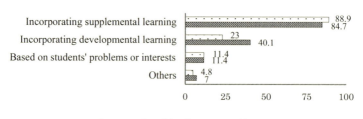

☐ Contents of teaching for team teaching
▨ Contents of teaching for small group teaching

(Ibid)

Finally, the actual counselling of students going to upper secondary or getting jobs after graduation should be mentioned. A lot of time is used for moral education based on career development after their graduation and around 90% of lower secondary schools provide opportunities like upper secondary visits, work experience, company visits, and volunteer activities. However nearly one fifth of students are not satisfied with the program and further improvements are required.

Fig. 1-3-4 Contents of Career and Academic Counselling (%)

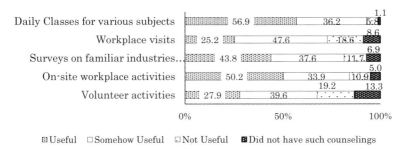

(National Institute for Educational Policy Research, *Comprehensive survey on career guidance and counseling*, 2013)

2. Summary of the Current System (Upper Secondary Schools)
(1) Purposes and objectives

After the World War II, upper secondary schools were established following lower secondary school education. In general, upper secondary has at least three years, four years if enrolled part time and students are required to acquire a certain number of credits for graduation. They are educational institutions equivalent to level 3 of the International Standard Classification of Education (ISCED). The ratio of enrollment in them is extremely high and they resemble semi-compulsory institutions.

The purpose of upper secondary school is to provide advanced general and specialized education in accordance with the mental and physical development and future course of students based on the education received in lower secondary schools.

Moreover, a upper secondary diploma is a basic qualification required for entrance to higher education institutions and employment. Each upper secondary school provides an individual curriculum in accordance with the course of study to realize its purpose and also recognizes the actual situation of students and their achievements.

(2) Various types

Depending on its foundation, upper secondary schools are categorized into three types, publicly established schools by prefectures and municipalities, private schools established by IEIs, and national schools attached to national universities which are maintained by university corporations. Additionally, private companies have recently established their own schools that are deemed private.

There are three types of upper secondary schools depending on how they provide lessons. For full-day courses, classes are held daytime, while evening courses are provided in the evening for 4-years. Students in correspondence courses learn through correspondence education mainly at home.

Upper secondary schools can be classified according to differences in acquiring credits as well. In the grade system, credits are allocated for each grade and students cannot acquire credits exceeding the number of grades allocated nor be promoted without accumulating a designated amount of credits. In the credit system, only a designated number of credits and at least 3 years of enrollment are required for graduation, and the usual grade system is not utilized.

There are a lot of courses in upper secondary schools and many upper secondary schools provide multiple courses. Apart from general courses, such variety lends itself to vocational education in technology, commerce, agriculture, homemaking, nursing, fishery, welfare, and information. Thus, specialized courses are designed to acquire skills directly connected to employment and in general these are called vocational upper secondary schools. In vocational courses, 30 or more credits are allocated to specialized subjects apart from basic subjects. However, vocational courses are not so popular and the number of students is declining. At present, new specialized courses not for vocational studies but for arts, sports and international studies related courses have opened. Furthermore other new courses mainly for advanced learning and inquiry-based learning are also provided for university entrance examinations and such courses have become popular among students.

On the other hand, other types of comprehensive courses are being provided to promote individualization and students are able to choose a certain number of subjects according their interests and aptitudes.

(3) Academic and career counseling/career education

In upper secondary schools, career education has been developed for students who will be employed just after graduation to inform them about industrial knowledge and guidance. Under such situations, the revised course of study of Upper Secondary School 2009 clearly requires all upper secondary schools to promote career education via a well-organized process of classroom activities as well as career counselling.

(4) Issues (upper secondary schools)

Although upper secondary schools initially started as comprehensive schools with general and vocational education, the system has diversified accordingly with the increase number of schools. As a result, the name upper secondary is just one, but their targets, quality of students, purposes and contents of education are far more different from each other at present.

Moreover, although it is said that there are diversified needs, there is still a deep-rooted preference in society for general upper secondary schools (Refer to **Fig. 1-3-5**). For instance, demand for vocational schools are low and, according to the School Basic Survey 2016, students in general courses accounted for over 70% compared to less than 20% (technical 7.7%, commerce 6.0%, agriculture 2.5% and homemaking 1.2%, nursing 0.4%, fishery 0.3%, welfare 0.3% and information 0.1%) in vocational courses. In addition, some students in vocational courses have less aspiration in general.

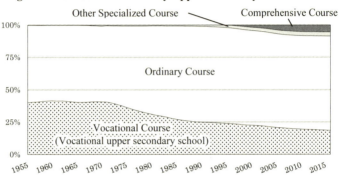

Fig. 1-3-5 Number of Students by Upper Secondary School Courses

(The author made originally, based on MEXT, The Basic Statistics of Schools: each year)

For the next course of study revisions which are currently under deliberation and scheduled to be implemented annually from 2022, new subjects including specific active learning courses will be introduced to realize a higher quality curriculum. It seems that future important issues regarding Japan's upper secondary education will be how the quality of education would be ensured or enhanced while taking into consideration the balance between "assurance of commonality" and "responses towards diversification" under the current situation where subject choices are increasing.

Column-2: Special Activities

1. Contents and Objectives

Special Activities are held within the formal curriculum as extra-curricular activities outside of the main subjects. After the war a subject called "free study" was set up as a trial course of study in 1947. The name of "special education activities" was adopted in 1958. Afterward the name was changed to "special activities" including school events in the courses of study publicly announced from 1968 to 1970.

In the present course of study, four main objectives are pointed out. First, to raise the mind, body, and individuality of each student through group activities. Second, to develop a voluntary and practical attitude contributing to a better life and human relationships as a member of group. Third, to respect the independent character of students. Fourth, to proceed learning focused on practical activities related to a better life. In a word those emphasized a whole-person education, collectivity, sociability, volunteer attitude, life-oriented education, and practical character.

It is important from the view of a whole-person education, that traditional education in Japan stresses sociability and relationship to community life as well as intellectual, moral and physical education.

2. TOKKATSU

Special activities with the characteristics mentioned above could be considered to be a kind of model of Japanese-type education. The Japanese government intends to inform foreign countries about special activities as "TOKKATSU". The countries that introduced this include Mongolia, Myanmar, India and Egypt. In particular, schools in those countries have an interest in group sweeping, school supplied lunches, various role plays, club activities, self-government activities, and group discipline of students.

Column-3: One Day in Lower Secondary School

The starting time of lower secondary school is about 8:30 a.m. Teachers check the day's schedule after arrival. When students arrive at school, teachers take notice of their appearance at the school gate, saying 'good morning'. After the starting time, a staff meeting is carried out, while students read books in the classrooms. Before class, homeroom teachers tell the students the daily schedule and grasp their physical condition.

Usually there are four classes in the morning, and two in the afternoon. It is a feature of lower secondary school that students have contact with many teachers because of the teaching subject system. Teachers spend any free time preparing teaching materials, marking exams, checking students' work and

Table 1-3-2

One Day in Lower Secondary School

8:35	Open
8:45 ~ 8:55	Homeroom
9:00 ~ 9:50	1st period
Recess (10min)	
10:00 ~ 10:50	2nd period
Recess (15min)	
11:00 ~ 11:50	3rd period
Recess (10min)	
12:00 ~ 12:50	4th period
Lunch Time (25min)	
Noon Recess (20min)	
13:40 ~ 14:30	5th period
Recess (10min)	
14:40 ~ 15:30	6th period
Cleaning (10min)	
Homeroom (10min)	
15:55 ~ 18:00	Club Activity

sometimes lecture students with bad behavior. Some schools serve school meals, but some districts do not and students have to bring their own lunch box. After the final lesson, cleaning and homeroom starts, where a homeroom teacher confirms the next day's schedule.

After school, most students participate in club activities to learn a sense of responsibility and togetherness. As such activities can become time consuming and burdensome for students and for teachers as well, a day-off system needs to be introduced. Teachers often have a meeting with their colleagues after school. They share information as to school events, extra-curricular activities, progress of students, and so on. Sometimes they cope with issues of parents or their community. After club activities, teachers help students get home promptly and safely, saying 'good bye' by the school gate. The closing time of lower secondary school is formally about 5:00 p.m., but many teachers work afterward.

Chapter 1. Schools 53

§4. Higher Education

1. Japanese Higher Education System
(1) Institutions for higher education

Institutions for higher education in Japan are universities (undergraduate and graduate school), junior colleges, colleges of technology (grades 4 and 5). Specialized training colleges and even colleges and academies under the jurisdiction of ministries other than the MEXT may also be included in this category as well. Universities have 4-year undergraduate programs (medical sciences etc. are a 6-year system), 2-year master's degree program, and 3 or 5-year doctor courses. Junior colleges are on a two or three-year system. Colleges of technology are five-year institutions beginning after lower secondary school and their first three years are in the secondary education stage while the other two years are deemed higher education. Specialized training colleges are also educational establishments that accept upper secondary graduates and many of them are on a one or two year course system. Colleges and academies which are outside the jurisdiction of MEXT vary, but for those who can award degrees are on a 4-year system equivalent to university. In this section, universities (including graduate schools) and junior colleges are mainly treated from the viewpoint of scale, history, and so on as they are the main institutions of the higher education system in Japan.

(2) Purpose and characteristics of each higher education institution

The purpose of each higher education institution is stipulated in the School Education Law (SEL). According to it, universities as a center of academy, aim to widely transfer knowledge, to deeply teach and research specialized fields. They must develop intellectual, moral, and applicable capabilities and contributions to the development of society by conducting education and research to realize these aims and provide the results to society. Focusing on its functional aspects, universities are characterized by their mission as education and research facilities as well as being required to contribute to society.

Junior colleges are viewed equally in the SEL in that they should deeply teach and research on specialized fields. Also, they need to foster the necessary skills for vocation or actual life and its course term shall be two or three years. Junior colleges are characterized by high practicality and their main function is to cultivate the necessary skills for vocational education and actual life.

The purpose of graduate schools are to teach and research on academic theory and its application, to extend its depth or to cultivate profound academic knowledge and outstanding ability to take professions that require a high level of expertise, and by this, contribute to the progress of culture. Obviously, graduate schools are expected to give and undertake a higher level of education and research than undergraduate courses. It becomes increasingly more important within the university as the academic research center. It has been increased in number due to the priority policy for graduate school which has been developed mainly at the former Imperial University since the 1990s. The main function of graduate schools had been the training of researchers, but in recent years professional graduate schools have been established to teach and research on academic theory and its application, to cultivate profound academic knowledge and outstanding ability in professions that require a high level of expertise.

2. Diversity of Institutions of Higher Education

Many upper secondary students go on to universities, junior colleges, or specialized training colleges after graduation. In general, the degree of difficulty to pass the university selective process is of the highest level, followed by junior and specialized training college. However, there can be recognized differences within each category, and such a trend is just a rough guideline.

Especially universities can vary widely. Japanese universities can be classified into three different providers: state, local government, and private corporations. In general, in order to go to university, the National Center Test for University Admission (NCTUA) is indispensable and private universities are ranked widely, from the highest ranked to those which students can easily access. Universities differ in size from nearly 67 thousand students to less than 300. Accordingly, faculty size can be numerous or limited to just one department. Some universities are for mainly science and engineering and others focus on the human and social sciences. There are universities with long traditions of more than 150 years and new ones with just a few years history.

3. Enrollment in Higher Education Institutions
(1) Entrance qualification

Entrance qualification for university and junior college is clearly described in the SEL as follows. Those who can enter university are those who graduated from upper secondary or secondary school or that those who completed ordinary twelve year school education (...), or those who are recognized by the MEXT as having academic ability equal to or higher than those mentioned above. For example, persons who have completed twelve years of school education in a foreign country, and students who completed the educational institution equivalent to this or who possesses its equivalent, students who completed the upper secondary courses of specialized training colleges, and those who passed the University Entrance Qualification Examination would fall under this category. Those who have completed ordinary twelve year school education include students from higher divisions of school for special needs education and 4th and 5th grade students from colleges of technology.

(2) Enrollment method

Japanese universities and junior colleges are able to decide the selection method for candidates according to the "the University Entrance Selection Execution Guidelines" issued by MEXT. As a result, methods differ significantly from one to another. However, as a general trend, it consists of a writing test of some subjects and other types of special entrance examinations (recommended entrance examinations, admission office entrance examinations, etc.)[8]. In recent years, due to the necessity of securing an adequate number of students which arose from the declining population of 18 years old, the proportion of enrollees in the special entrance examination is increasing especially at private universities, and 40% of university entrants are successful candidates for special entrance examinations. However, according to the above "Guidelines", the upper limit is set at 50% of the enrollment number.

Various types of selective processes have been developed among universities and this trend can be recognized even in one university depending on the sort of faculty. Only the case of the general entrance examination for 4 year universities is explained below. Such selective method largely differs between national universities, universities provided by the local government, and private universities. In order to go to a national university or university provided by the local government, candidates must take the NCTUA (in January) as the first step and afterward, they have to take the entrance examinations of each university they wish to attend (from the end of February to the beginning of March). Some of them change universities according to their university test scores and NCTUA results. Private universities usually implement their own academic tests, but some of them utilize the NCTUA.

---

8 Hirotaka Nanbu, *Undergraduate and Graduate Admission Systems in East Asia* (in Japanese), Toshindo, 2016.

Pic.1-4-1 One Scene of NCTUA

(Held in a university lecture room in January)

(3) Trend of admission to higher education

The 18-year-old population, the minimum age of university admission, has declined from the peak of 2.7 million in 1992, to about 1.2 million in recent years, which is less than half of the peak. This figure will continue to decrease and it is estimated that it will be less than 1 million in 2031. Comparing 1992 and 2014, the number of university and junior college students has decreased from 790,000 to 680,000. It is clear that this rate of decrease is much smaller than that of the rate of decrease in the 18-year-old population which implies the percentage of students seeking a higher education grew. The current rate is close to 60%. In more detail, the number of those who advanced to a four year university has increased from 540,000 to 620,000 between 1992 and 2014, while in the case of junior colleges it has decreased sharply from 250,000 to 60,000. Furthermore, the number of those enrolled in specialized training colleges has decreased from 360,000 to 260,000.

While the total number of student entering university is decreasing, some universities continue to enjoy a highly competitive enrollment, on the other hand, many other universities have failed to make their quota. It is said that 40%

of private universities, mainly in rural areas, are in such a situation. Since the 1990s, the number of female students going to a four year university has increased and many junior colleges where over 90% of the students were girls have been reorganized into four year universities. The number of junior colleges has decreased sharply from about 600 in 1990 to about 350 in 2015.

In recent years, the number of students from abroad has increased because of the progress of globalization and the promotion of internationalization of higher education. The number of international students enrolled in higher education in Japan has increased significantly from about 40,000 in 1990 to about 150,000 in 2015. For universities, accepting these students is also a countermeasure against a declining birth rate.

4. Education in Higher Education Institutions
(1) Faculty and department

In universities and junior colleges, education in humanities, social science, natural science, agriculture, medicine and dentistry, health, home economics, pedagogy, arts and other disciplines is provided. Regarding four year universities as a whole, majoring in social science is most popular (32%), followed by engineering (15%), humanities science (14%) and health (10%). However, course contents vary widely depending on the provider. In national universities, the proportion of humanities and social science majors are the lowest. On the contrary, a high proportion can be recognized in natural science, engineering, agriculture, medicine and dentistry. These fields cover about the half of education area of national universities and proportion of educational studies is also relatively high. In universities provided by local governments, the ratio of humanities and social science majors is high. Moreover, the proportion of health sector majors is higher compared with others, probably due to the recently established universities and faculties of health care and nursing. In private universities, humanities and social sciences represent more than half of all majors. Especially, the ratio of social science majors is more than two-thirds of the total. Science and teacher training whose education costs are high are provided for by national universities while private universities offer education mainly in the field of social science which is cheaper and is suitable for mass-production education.

Regarding junior colleges, it is remarkable that the proportion of educational studies (37.6%) and home economics (18.5%) majors is higher compared to four year universities. But those numbers differ largely between local governmental and private junior colleges. The former has the highest percentage of majors in social science (30.1%), followed by humanities science (23.3%), home economics (20.1%), and educational studies (8.1%). In the private sector, educational studies majors account for about 40% (39.3%), followed by home economics (18.4%), and health (9.9%). The percentage of humanities and social science majors, which is top among the local governmental junior colleges, is 8.6% and 7.7% respectively- in terms of ranking, these are fourth and fifth. Being that educational studies holds a large proportion in private junior colleges, seems to indicate that they mainly attract students who are likely to acquire teacher qualifications.[9]

(2) Course after graduation

75% of university graduates and 79% of junior college graduates find jobs after graduation. Their job placement varies according to which higher education institution they attended and their specialized field. Many of them are employed by private companies, but others become civil servants, teachers and so on. Those who continue their studies at a senior educational institution are 11% and 10% respectively. These figures also vary largely depending on which higher education institution they attended and their specialized field. In the case of the universities, the rate of students who enter graduate schools for natural sciences and engineering is higher than humanities and social science.

---

9   All data from MEXT, *Statistical Handbook on Education*, 2016 edition.

Generally, university students and junior college students graduate in March and start working in April. Job hunting activities generally begin a year and a half before graduation although it varies somewhat depending on the year. The peak of job hunting is the summer before graduation. The employment rate in 2015 was 97.3% for university graduates and 97.4% for junior college graduates. The employment rate depends on the economic situation, but when its rate becomes lower, such a situation could be a social problem. When job hunting activities are prolonged, it might have a serious influence on university education, such as absence of classes.

(3) Enhancement of university education

Today, the quality guaranteed of higher education is a universal topic including Japan. Under the slogan of shifting from teaching to learning in recent decades, higher education reforms are progressing in a direction that emphasizes what students have learned. Various improvements concerning higher education are being carried out, under the initiative of the MEXT: for example, fulfillment of syllabus, creation of numbering, creation of a course tree, and enhancement of the guidance system of students and so on. These are often referred to as indexes of university assessment and application requirements for competitive funds.

In addition, the Regulative Standards for University Establishment stipulates that universities shall implement systematic training and research to improve the content and methods of their lessons. In this way, implementation of Faculty Development (FD) is mandated. Its expansion has been strongly promoted as an educational policy. FD is generally regarded as an effective activity to enhance the educational potential in Japan. In recent years, active learning has been recommended. Instead of doing one way lectures, educational methods that students can learn actively are required. Although it cannot be said that it is already mainstream, but various efforts are being made at many universities and their departments.

5. Higher Education Expenses
(1) Tuition and scholarships

One of the characteristic aspects of Japanese higher education in terms of educational expenses is the high personal expenses. The average total enrollment fee and tuition for 4 years at a private university costs about 3.6 million yen: converted at 110 yen per dollar, it is about US$ 33,000, and converted at 120 yen per euro, it is about €30,000 (FY 2015). Of course, there is a difference not only between universities but also between fields. Tuition fees in the fields of humanities and social sciences are generally less expensive than those of natural sciences and engineering. Costs for the faculty of medicine are even more expensive. In the case of national and universities provided by local governments, although cheaper than private universities, the amount is still about 2.4 million yen (about US$22,000 €20,000). As teaching materials and living expenses are added to this, the financial burden of students and their families is enormous. Many students rely on the parents and a part-time job to cover tuition fees and living expenses and as a result, a lot of problems such as reflecting economic disparity and reduction in learning time are occurring.

Compared to such expensive tuition fees, the scholarship system in Japan is not substantial. The main scholarship in Japan is the scholarship of the Japan Student Services Organization (JASSO). JASSO's scholarship is a loan and thus comes with the obligation to pay it back. Also, the loan amount is insufficient, making it difficult to even cover tuition fees. Students can receive additional loans, but of course the amount that must be paid back increases accordingly. In recent years, due to the development of a disparate society, the existence of those who abandon continuing their studies at higher education institutions for economic reasons has become a serious social problem, and the mass media often reports on it. In order to cope with such a situation, a benefit scholarship was newly introduced by JASSO in April 2017. The amount of benefit is 20,000 to 40,000 yen a month, which alone cannot cover the expenses necessary for continuing studies at a university. While state finances are in a difficult situation, how to fund social resources is a big issue.

(2) University operating expenses

A large amount of expenditure is needed to maintain a university. Focusing on its income, its structure is very different among the three types of universities.

The major income for private universities is student payments (tuition fee etc.), accounting for 3/4 of their entire income. However, subsidies for private schools (including universities) are paid from public expenditure, because private schools play an important role in spreading and promoting educational opportunities in Japan. The actual subsidy amount is about 10% of current account expenses and is gradually decreasing due to financial difficulties.

The national universities and universities managed by local governments previously operated almost all of their expenses using public funds, but in 2004 all national universities became incorporated and management efforts were required of them. For the university operated by the local government, a similar system was also introduced in 2004 and in fiscal year 2016 approximately 3/4 of them are incorporated. Among the income of national universities, the largest is university grants and various subsidies which are from the state budget. They account for about 2/3 of their total income, followed by the income of the tuition and admission fee at about 15%, and about 18% from so-called external funds: figures excluding revenues from university attached hospital. For national universities, university grants, which are not for any specified state expenditures, accounts for about half of the total income, but it has been reduced by the fixed rate (about 1%) every year. For this reason, national universities are forced to acquire competitive funds.

Since the 1990s, prioritized financial support by competitive funds has been implemented for all universities. 21st Century COE (Center of Excellence) Program (2002), Global COE Program that succeeded it (2007), Support Program for Distinctive University Education (2003), Support Program for

Contemporary Educational Needs (2004), and the Education Promotion Program for Workers Recurrent Education Needs (2007) were launched. Recently, in order to strengthen research universities, "Top Global University Project" (2014) is being implemented.

However, acquisition of funds is a very important problem for each university in any case. For this reason, it has been pointed out that incorporation to encourage liberty, creativity and innovation, on the contrary, binds university activities.

§5. Special Needs Education

1. Development of Inclusive Education in Japan

The education system for children with disabilities was partially reformed in 2006 and the new system named "Special Needs Education (SNE)" started. The Fundamental Law of Education (FLE) was partially amended to introduce new articles on Special Needs Education for the first time. Article 4-2 of FLE reads "The government and local society must propose educational support for people with disabilities in consideration of their individual disabilities and educational needs."

Former special schools, which had been provided separately by type of disability, as "Schools for the Blind", "Schools for the Deaf", "Schools for the Intellectually Disabled, the Physically Disabled and the Health Impaired", have been unified and renamed "Schools for Special Needs Education (Schools for SNE)." One particular school for SNE can accept students with several types of disabilities.

This reform is active under the principle of "Inclusive Education" that aims to promote an inclusive society. In the Inclusive education system, children with disabilities and non-disabled children learn together. That means, children with disabilities are not excluded from the general education system on the basis of disability and can access a general education on an equal basis with others in the communities in which they live while reasonable accommodation is provided to person with disabilities (article 24, "Convention on the Rights of Person with Disabilities").

Under the principle, educational services should be prepared based on "personal" or "individual needs", not on "places" or "impairment." So, special educational support should be provided not only for children settled in SNE schools or special classes, but also in regular classes of regular schools need to be considered the needs of appropriate instruction. To meet such needs of children with disabilities, Individualized Teaching Plans (ITP) and Individualized Education Support Plans (IESP) are prepared.

An ITP stipulates the teaching contents and methods for each child. It is made by school teachers. IESP provide appropriate long-term support from infancy to employment in cooperation with not only schools, but welfare, medical, health, and labor related organizations.

Now the SNE system is on progress to expand targets of ITP or IESP and requires a Special Needs Education Coordinator (SENCO) at each school. MEXT took advantage of creating a co-living society and suggested it quite a big role of Special Needs education ("Promotion of Special Needs Education" 2007.) The Central Council for Education (CCE) made cognition of the vision of Inclusive education ("Promotion of Special Needs Education for Construction of Inclusive Education System for Creation of Co-Living Society", 2012.)

In 2016, the Act to Advance the Elimination of Discrimination based on Handicap has been enforced and it requires stricter prohibition of discrimination connected to any disabilities and reasonable accommodation should be prepared for them.

Table 1-5-1 Development of Special Needs Education System

1993	Resource Rooms System started
2003	The Future of Special Needs Education (CCE report)
2004	The act of support for developmental disabilities
2006	Amendment of FLE and SEL
2007	Promotion of Special Needs Education (MEXT)
2012	Promotion of Special Needs Education for the construction of an inclusive education system for creating a co-living society (CCE report)
2016	The Act to Advance the Elimination of Discrimination based on Disabilities

2. The Present Status of SNE for Children with Disabilities

SNE for children with disabilities is now carried out in various forms in Japan, such as schools for SNE, special classes, and resource rooms of regular schools.

According to a survey regarding special needs education, the ratio of children formally provided SNE totaled 2.8% (1.3% in special classes of regular schools, 0.9% was in schools for SNE, and 0.6 % joined resource rooms.) The ratio becomes higher at compulsory education (3.6% of primary and lower secondary education combined)

(1) Schools for special needs education (schools for SNE)

Schools for SNE established for children with comparatively severe disabilities of blindness and low vision, deaf and hard-of-hearing, intellectual disabilities, physical disabilities, and health impairments should have an primary department, lower secondary department, and may have a kindergarten department and a upper secondary department (including schools with a hospital attached). The standard class size is six. The upper secondary department has eight students per class. Class size for classes with students with multiple disabilities is three.

In 2014, there were 1,125 schools for SNE (45 national, 1067 district, 13 private), 11 more than the previous year. The number of children in such schools was 139,821 (1,927 increased from the previous year). It looks irregular that annually the numbers of schools and children in schools for SNE are both increasing while the total number of children enrolled is decreasing in Japan.

(2) Special classes

Special classes are for children with comparatively mild disabilities that may be provided in regular primary and upper secondary schools (they may also be established as branch classes in a hospital). These classes are for children with vision or hearing impairments, intellectual disabilities, physical disabilities, health impairments, speech impairments, autism and emotional disturbances.

The standard class size is eight (three in the case of multiple disabilities) , relatively better conditions compared to the ordinary class size of 40. As of 2014, the number of special classes in primary schools was 39,386 (2,026 annual increase) and in lower secondary schools 17,840 (annual increase of 580) . At the same time, the number of ordinary classes has decreased, so it seems obvious that special educational supports are required.

The increasing number of schools, classes, and children for SNE appears to contradict the principle of Inclusive education. It could be caused by an increasing of number of children with multiple and more severe disabilities (which means more specific supports are needed), or increasing of numbers of children with developmental disabilities who should be taken care of in regular classes (which means there are no space for children with more severe disabilities), or a decrease in discrimination against those with disabilities (which means it is easier to choose/accept special classes or schools for SNE for parents.)

(3) Resource rooms

Children with disabilities who are enrolled in and studying most of the time in regular classes may visit resource rooms a few times a week to receive special instruction.

In regular classes, according to the survey for school teachers in 2012, the estimated percentage of children who are not impaired intellectually but have developmental disabilities (Learning Disability: LD, Attention Deficit / Hyperactive Disorder: ADHD, Autistic Syndrome etc.) and have special educational needs is 6.3%. Then it becomes a legal obligation to treat them properly in all regular classes considering their individual educational needs. So now, resource room programs cover disabilities such as speech impairment, autism, emotional disturbance, low vision, hard-of-hearing, LD, ADHD, and others. Some of them go to another school's resource room to get special instructions.

(4) The Course of Study for schools for SNE

According to the course of study for schools for SNE, aside from education conforming to kindergarten, primary, lower secondary, and upper secondary education, a special guidance course to improve and overcome the difficulties associated with disabilities is taught (it is called "self-reliance activities") at schools for SNE and the curriculum can also be arranged to suite the child's disability condition (Several subjects may be integrated or a younger-aged curriculum may be adopted).

"Self-reliance activities" consist of six skills (maintenance of health, psychological stability, construction of human relationships, cognition of environment, physical movement, and communication) and instruction suited to each disability is prepared.

(5) SENCO (Special Educational Needs Coordinator)

All schools should have SENCO and in 2013, 87.1% schools already had such staff (95.1% of local kindergartens and 99.9% of local primary and secondary schools have SENCOs). The roles of a SENCO are arranged by the school commission for Special Education Needs (SEN), cooperation with parents or institutes outside of the school, co-working with teachers and so on. There are cases that the school principal, vice-principal, or special classes' teachers function as the SENCO. In such cases, they could cope with the tasks because of their position or knowledge of school children, but at the same time they tend to be too busy to attend to the whole school special educational needs properly.

3. Future Problems of SNE : Enrollment and Teachers
(1) Enrollment

The type of education appropriate for a child with a disability is recommended by the municipal advisory committee on school attendance based on the health examination children must take before they enter primary school. The municipal board of education then gives this recommendation to the prefectural board of education. The prefectural board of education makes a decision considering the child's disabilities and educational needs, parents' needs, and opinions from educational, medical, and psychological staff. Children admitted to SNE schools are called "admitted person to schools for SEN." The parents, child, school teachers, and the board of education should all agree on the final decision.

Today it is very important to think about what is best for the child. Which school the child should go is decided under reasonable accommodation of individual requirements and long-term instruction (infancy to employment) is provided to maximize the academic and social development of the child.

(2) Teachers of special needs education

In addition to a regular teacher's license of kindergarten, primary, or secondary school, a teacher who works for schools for SNE should be licensed to teach at schools for SNE. 70% teachers in schools for SEN have both licenses which mean 30% do not. In general schools (they do not need to have license of schools for SNE) 70% do not have a SEN school license. That means, in several schools or classes, teachers may not have special knowledge or special skills to teach children with disabilities, and may manage with only on-the-job training.

The government encourages teachers to get a license for schools for SNE by taking the Educational Personnel Exam. Many lectures are provided by colleges or local education boards to support them.

Under the principle of the new system, inclusive education, it is now strongly required that school teachers have knowledge and skills to teach students with disabilities and special support is provided at all schools.

§6. Specialized Training College and Miscellaneous Schools

1. Outline and Aims of These Schools

Primary or lower secondary schools are regulated as formal schools in article 1 of the School Education Law (SEL). It also defines specialized training colleges as institutions that develop vocational and practical skills and knowledge, and miscellaneous schools as institutions that provide education equivalent to formal schools. But these schools vary widely in the length of study and size and they are not considered as formal schools. That is the reason why such schools are regulated as a different type of school.

In the prewar period, "miscellaneous school" meant all schools except formal schools. For example, kindergartens were regarded as a kind of miscellaneous school because they were absent of any regulation to provide a sufficient education to children. In the beginning when the SEL launched, such a dated way of thinking was succeeded. But among these schools, some institutions began to educate more students in a better-prepared environment for a longer period of time than before. Then, the Ministry of Education changed the policy and reformed the law to categorize specialized training colleges as quasi legitimate institutions in the SEL in 1975.

At that time, specialized training colleges were regulated as follows.

1. Period of study: more than 1 year
2. Number of school hours: more than 800 hours per year (in the case of evening classes: more than 450 hours per year)
3. Number of students: more than 40

Other precise provisions were described in Ministry of Education ordinances.

2. Entrance Requirements and Course Terms

Since there is no legal regulation as to the qualifications for admission, it is decided by each miscellaneous school. Although the term of study is generally stipulated as over one year, there is an exception that the learning period can be modified to three or more or one year or less in the case of schools of arts and crafts.

Specialized training colleges can provide upper secondary, postsecondary and general courses. Students leaving from compulsory schools can enter the upper secondary course. Entering postsecondary courses requires a certificate of the completion of secondary school. A specialized training college which has upper secondary courses can be called an Upper Secondary Specialized Training School, and a school providing postsecondary courses may be referred to as a Professional Training College. The term of study for specialized training colleges is one year or more and there is no upper limit. Some colleges have 4-year programs.

3. Various Type of the Specialized Training Colleges and Miscellaneous Schools

Fig. 1-6-1 shows the change of the number of specialized training colleges and miscellaneous schools and **Fig. 1-6-2** indicates the change in the number of students at these schools.

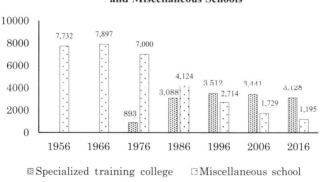

Fig. 1-6-1 Number of Specialized Training Colleges and Miscellaneous Schools

(MEXT, School Basic Survey)

From the end of the World War II to the 1960s, there were numerous miscellaneous schools in Japan but many these schools were reorganized into specialized training colleges by the revision of the SEL in 1975. Since then, the number of miscellaneous schools has been declining consistently and at present, the number of these schools is nearly 1/7 of its peak, and the number of students is about 1/12 as well.

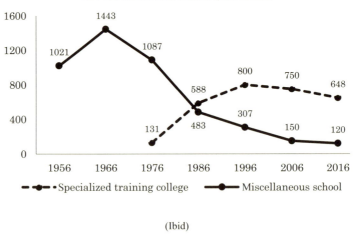

Fig. 1-6-2 The Number of Student in Specialized Training College and Miscellaneous School (thousand)

(Ibid)

In spite of the decline of miscellaneous schools, specialized training colleges increased until the 1980s. But subsequently, the number of colleges and students reached its peak in mid 90s and has gradually decreased since then.

Let's look at the numerical analysis of specialized training college students by their specialty. The medical course to become hospital staff like nurses or physical therapists is the most common. It occupies a third of the whole. The next largest courses are technological coaching for computer engineers, hygienic education to become hairdressers or cooks, and commercial training such as bookkeeping. Each course occupies 10% of the whole. From this data, it can be recognized that specialized training colleges have made efforts in vocational education. Currently, the period for most vocational education tends to be extended. Therefore, for example, upper secondary specialized training schools for licensed practical nurses or enrolled nurses are decreasing.

In the miscellaneous school system, one-fourth of all students are studying in a driving school or a foreign school and about 20% of their students are attending preparatory schools for university entrance examinations. In addition, international schools, Japanese language schools and Korean schools are included in foreign schools.

4. Entrance to Specialized Training Colleges and Aquirable Qualifications

In Japan because most students go to upper secondary schools, and only 0.3% of graduates of compulsory education enter upper secondary specialized training courses (including general courses). But like upper secondary schools, completing 3 years of upper secondary specialized training can qualify graduates for university admission.

Professional training colleges holding postsecondary courses can offer higher levels of vocational education since they admit upper secondary graduates. Therefore, the student can obtain various qualifications according to their specialty. For example, the certifications of assistant surveyor, dietitian, cooks, childcare worker and care worker are given after completing each vocational training course. In case of car mechanics, general nurses, medical technologists, and hairdressers, students will be able to take the state examination for each certification when they finish their training program.

Professional training colleges that have more than 2-years of upper secondary courses and meet certain conditions may grant postsecondary course diplomas and graduates of these colleges can transfer to university. Furthermore, advanced diplomas and qualifications for admission to graduate school are given to graduates who have successfully completed over 4-years of upper secondary courses outline in the regulations.

5. Advantages and Problems of these Schools

Specialized training colleges and miscellaneous schools have an advantage over other schools because they can easily change the school size, the curriculum and the term of study depending on the vocational needs under modern society where the skills required for employment change in a short time. Common corporations and private individuals other than national, local governments, and IEIs, also can establish these schools. It makes providing flexible education more possible.

On the other hand, it is of concern that management of schools administrated by common corporations or private individuals could become unstable. Actually there are many inactive specialized training colleges and miscellaneous schools in Japan. Several schools appropriateness as an educational institution has been called into question. Management and Coordination Agency has counseled the Ministry of Education to improve student recruiting, curriculum, and the environment of these schools.

From now on, it is more necessary to consider eliminating the different treatments between these schools and other schools regulated in Article 1 of the SEL. As a formality there is the entering or transfer path from specialized training colleges to university. But if miscellaneous schools students want to enter the university, these schools have to individually obtain authorization from the Ministry of Education and students in such miscellaneous schools cannot apply for Japan Student Services Organization scholarships. How to occupy a position of specialized training college and miscellaneous school which can provide flexible education in the legitimate school system is a future problem.

Column-4: Cram Schools (Juku)

Cram schools, called "Gakushu Juku" or simply Juku, are special private schools that offer after-school supplementary lessons or advanced lessons. According to the research of MEXT in 2007, mathematics and Japanese language are the most popular among primary school students and mathematics and English among lower and upper secondary students.

That research revealed that about 25.9% of primary school students and 53.5% of lower and upper secondary students went to Juku in 2007, while 16.5% and 44.5% respectively in 1985. It means that the proportion of children who go to Juku has increased and their age has decreased for twenty years. One of the main reasons for the increased popularity of Juku is the declining quality of public education and the higher attention for education among parents. Parents tend to think that public education is not enough to pass entrance exams and desire to give their children a better education from an earlier age to get a head start on the possibility of going to a better school. However, the cost is not small.

The average fee for Juku in 2007 was 11,988 yen (US$109) a month for the lower grades of primary school, 18,472 yen (US$167) for the upper grades of primary school, and 26,064 yen (US$236) for junior and upper secondary. This means not all families can afford to have their children go to Juku even if they wish. Especially, it is rather difficult for low-income families. Hence, the decrease in opportunities for children from low income families to learn is becoming a serious problem.

It is true that Juku has contributed to the academic progress of Japanese children in the form of supplementing public education in the past, but it has also caused inequity in education between low-income families and other families. To solve this problem, some local municipalities provide a free study program for children whose family cannot afford to let their children go to Juku.

Chapter 2. Curriculum Standards

1. Curriculum and its Standards

Curriculum is the school educational plan on which the educational contents are organized in relation to school days and hours. It is based on the development of students' mind and body and to realize the educational objectives and goals of the school.

Curriculum has the following standards. Firstly, at national level, the School Education Law (SEL) makes it clear that the Minister of Education has the final authority to decide the outline of curriculum from kindergarten to upper secondary. In addition, article 52 of its Ordinance for Enforcement shows the courses of study of each stage of school which is the curriculum standard. At the local level, article 21 of the Law Concerning Organization and Operation of Local Education Administration (LCOOLEA) stipulates that the board of education deals with curriculum, textbook, and other teaching materials Article 33 of the same law provides the board of education control over curriculum and teaching materials, etc. of schools in that area. Thus, prefectural and municipal boards of education play an essential role in the standard of education.

On the other hand, each school can organize its own curriculum under such regulations according to local circumstances. However, the principal of the school is asked to undertake it with the consent and cooperation of the staff concerned.

The curriculum is composed of three elements; school educational target, organization of educational contents, and the allocation of school days and hours. Firstly, the school educational target needs to follow two points. One is the target to maintain and improve the educational standards according to the national level under the Constitution of Japan, Fundamental Law of Education (FLE), SLE and its Ordinance for Enforcement and Courses of Study. The other one is the original target of each school based on the circumstances in and around that school.

Secondly, this Ordinance provides educational contents for each level of school. For example, the course of study of primary school, which was revised on March 2017, consists of such subjects as Japanese language, social studies, arithmetic, science, living environment studies, music, art and handicraft, home economics, physical education, foreign language, and moral education as a special subject. In addition, foreign Language activities, time for integrated studies, and extra-curricular activities are asked to be undertaken. Thirdly, Courses of Study provides the precise hours of each class and number of school days in a year based on the Ordinance for Enforcement (cf. Chapter 1, §2. Primary Education).

2. Courses of Study and their Transition

Courses of Study as standard of curriculum are issued by MEXT for kindergartens, primary, lower secondary, upper secondary and special education schools. It is also the criteria when textbooks are compiled and for activities in each school. The contents of education reflect the social needs and at the same time, it affects people's way of thinking and behavior in the near future.

The course of study was first launched after the World War II, and it has been revised about every 10 years. The first one was issued in 1947 as "referred to be consulted for teachers". They were compiled based on Empiricism and the model was the Courses of Study in the state of Virginia in the United States. This phrase, "tentative plan" continued to the following edition in 1951. The Courses of Study at that period were not treated as the basis of curriculum but just to be used as a reference.

However, in the revision of the course of study of upper secondary social studies in 1955, the word "tentative" was deleted and a few years later in 1958, when the new version for primary school and lower and upper secondary school was issued, it was announced as an official notification from the MECCS. The ministry insisted that the Courses of Study were the national standards of curriculum and schools had a legal obligation to obey. At that time, moral education was introduced and the educational concept changed from empiricism to systematics. In the next revision in 1968, "Modernization of education" was emphasized and the hours allotted to science education and other lessons were consequently increased. But, these two revisions were criticized as "cramming". As a result, when revised in 1977, the policy for a "less strenuous", "careful selective" education were emphasized, and educational contents and yearly school hours were decreased. In the 1988 revision, science and social studies for the lower grades in primary school were integrated into Living Environment Studies. Ten years later, the revisions aimed to nurture in students a "zest for living", The 5-day school week and a "more relaxed" education, a 30% reduction in educational content, and "period for integrated study", etc. were introduced. But, these Courses of Study were partly revised in 2003 because of the criticism against the lower standards of academic performance in general. The Ministry explained that the contents were changed and should be viewed as minimum standards which each school should implement.

The 2008 revision of Courses of Study took place in accordance with the revisions of FLE and SEL. In this case, to nurture the spirit of a "zest for living", balance between acquiring basic, fundamental knowledge and skills and fostering the ability to think, to make suitable decisions and express oneself, and the nurturing of a rich heart and healthy body were emphasized. In March 2015, the Ordinance for Enforcement of SEL were revised to change Moral Education to "Special subject: Morality", and then the Courses of Study for primary school, lower secondary school and those departments of special education schools were also partially revised.

In the latest March 2017 revision that will begin in the 2020 academic year, the policy to nurture a "zest for living", introduced in the 1998 revision, is still being emphasized. For this policy, 1) knowledge and skills, 2) the ability to think, make decision, and express oneself, 3) the ability to learn by oneself and humanity are emphasized. Each school needs to do characteristic and original educational activities through the improvement of classes to ensure that students "learn independently, interactively and deeply". Each school also needs to build up "Curriculum Management" mentioned later. Additionally, the new subject, "Foreign Language" was introduced into the upper grades of primary school. (cf. Table 1-2-1)

3. Textbook System
(1) The structure of the textbook system

There are two types of textbooks. One is a textbook approved by the Minister of Education and the other is one compiled by the Ministry itself. The SEL requires that all schools shall use either of them. But, upper secondary and special education schools can use other books as a textbook if they cannot find a proper one. Fig. 2-1 shows the process from the compilation of textbooks by the publisher to distributing them to students (this chart was made by the author, based on the homepage of Ministry of Education).

Fig.2-1 Current Distribution System of Textbooks

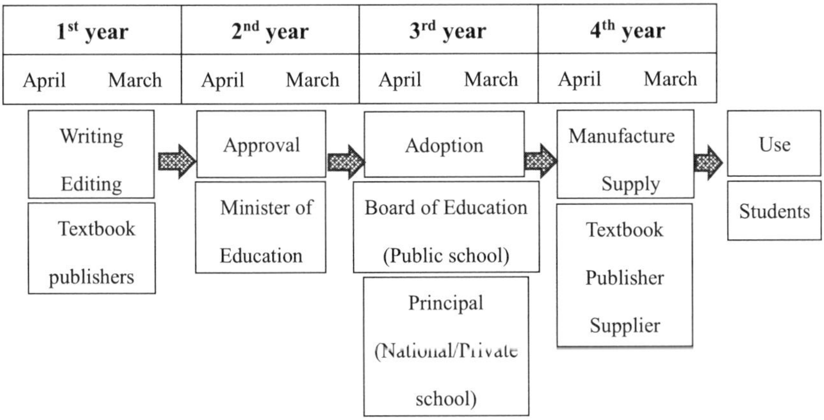

1st year		2nd year		3rd year		4th year		
April	March	April	March	April	March	April	March	
Writing Editing		Approval		Adoption		Manufacture Supply		Use
Textbook publishers		Minister of Education		Board of Education (Public school)		Textbook Publisher Supplier		Students
				Principal (National/Private school)				

(Source: Prepared by author)

The textbooks used in compulsory schools including state and private schools are handed out to all students free of charge by the central government, based on Article 26 of the Constitution of Japan.

The Ministry of Education introduced the new policy regarding "Digital textbooks" or tablet computers to all primary, lower secondary and upper secondary schools from the 2020 academic year. But in the present textbook system mentioned above, this "Digital textbook" is thought of as a teaching aid and Ministry of Education is going to revise the law. Although the law requires that textbooks shall be free during compulsory education, the large cost of implementation is a serious problem. How local governments should offset the cost of introducing tablet computers and whether parents should pay for it or not are the major concern.

(2) Textbook approval system

After the World War II, the former system on which textbooks had been issued by the central government since 1903 was replaced by the present approval system. This is the same system mentioned above in which the Minister of Education examines textbook drafts compiled by private publishers and checks whether their contents are in alignment with the course of study etc. The textbooks are approved or not by the Minister based on the recommendation of the Textbook Approval Council which is sought to ensure that textbooks meet educational requirements.

The purpose of the textbook approval system is to maintain and improve national educational standards and to keep neutrality in education. On the other hand, there have been a lot of people complaining about this system because it is direct intervention by the central government to the quality of educational contents. As one good example, some people including Saburo Ienaga had appealed to the court for almost 30 years from 1967 to ask how far the government should be involved in textbook approval and the range of the government's responsibility to education. Furthermore, from the point of people's fundamental right to education, such approval procedures which might be against the prohibition on censorship (Article 21) and academic freedom

Chapter 2. Curriculum Standards 81

(Article 23) guaranteed by the Constitution of Japan were also in dispute.

(3) Textbook adoption

It is the duty of prefectural or municipal boards of education to provide local schools and the principals of public and private schools the authority to adopt textbooks for their schools. The Law concerning Measures for Free Provision of Textbooks in Compulsory Education Schools provides the procedure to adopt textbooks used in primary, lower and first half of unified secondary schools and those departments of special education schools. The textbooks used in upper secondary are adopted by the board of education based on the actual situation of the school.

Each prefectural board of education sets regional divisions for adopting textbooks and the municipal boards of education decide on one text for each subject for that area. Each prefectural board of education sets up a Council for Textbook Selection to examine and research textbooks and give guidance, advice and support to municipal boards of education and principals of state and private schools in regards to textbooks.

4. Curriculum Management in School

The concept of Curriculum Management has been part of educational policy since its introduction in the 2000's. When the Courses of Study were revised in early 2017, every school was required to make it. Schools are expected to manage themselves independently and creatively in accordance with the actual state of their students and community and curriculum management plays leading role in school management. On the other hand, it is also required for schools to arrange suitable circumstances for making curriculum management effective.

It means to accomplish the target of education in each school systematically based on the Plan, Do, Check and Act (PDCA) cycle. That process includes 1) to fix the school educational targets and to organize the curriculum for it, 2) to conduct class effectively, 3) to assess class results, 4) to assess and improve the learning units, 5) to assess and improve teaching plans, 6) to assess curriculum contents, 7) to assess the school as a whole, 8) to start to improve, 9) to make up the targets and plans once again.[10]

The Curriculum Management is an organizational process carried out for the purpose of achieving school educational targets, then, assessing and improving those educational activities. Through Curriculum Management, all teachers and staff are going to share school educational targets, to do their educational activities systematically, to achieve the targets, to assess those educational activities and then to improve school educational targets and curriculum the following year. From this view point, it has a very important meaning to encourage school improvement systematically and continuously.

---

10   Shigeru Amagasa, *School Management based on Curriculum* (in Japanese), Gyosei, 2013, pp.24-25.

Column-5: The System and Situation of Students Promotion in School

Article 57 of the Ordinance for Enforcement of the SEL outlines promotion in primary education, and is applied to secondary education as well; "On the occasion of primary schools' approval of students' completion of the course program or their graduation, primary schools should take students' school achievements into account." Therefore, schools in primary and secondary education may require students to stay in the same class for another year when students do not satisfy school achievement criteria.

However, even though the ordinance allows schools to make students repeat the same grade, this rarely happens, especially in compulsory education. For example, there is a case where guardians contested the school's decision to promote their child after the student's long absence. The local court supported the school's decision and ruled in favor of the student's promotion (Kobe local court, 1993). On the other hand, in upper secondary, grade repetition is not relatively rare, and 13,610 students (0.4% of all upper secondary students in Japan) repeated the same grade in 2015. In any case, the number of students in Japan that repeat the same grade is less than other nations. Japanese schools may legislatively make their students repeat the same grade, but actually are run on an automatic promotion system.

Although grade repetition does happen in Japan, in general, grade-skipping is not permitted. There are exceptionally rare cases when early entrance to university after completion of the second grade of upper secondary school and early entrance to graduate school after completion of the third grade of university (Article 90 and 120 of SEL) are permitted. But in 2017, only 9 among 38 faculties at 6 universities permitted early entrance. From this, early entrance is rarely implemented in Japan.

Chapter 3. School Management

1. Background of School Management
(1) Educational administration by local educational authorities

In Japan, to ensure that schools are public in general, founders of schools are constrained to the national government, local governments (prefectural/ municipal governments), and incorporated educational institutions. Under the School Education Law (SEL), these founders have administrative authority over the schools they founded. In the case of primary and secondary public schools, under the SEL and the Law concerning Organization and Operation of Local Educational Administration (LCOOLEA), local public bodies establish school administrative organizations called boards of education and delegate to them the actual running of schools (personnel/ property/ operational management).

Thus, in the case of public schools, each board of education has the power and responsibility over general school management. However, the LCOOLEA provides that boards of education can formulate so-called "regulation of school management" specifying the board and the school's authorities and responsibilities over the school's basic management and operation, as well as over various clerical matters. Under the leadership of principals that have supervisory authority granted by the SEL, each school carries out their work with a certain degree of autonomy over administrative matters entrusted to them by the regulation of the local board of education, over matters that are stipulated in national law, and ordinances under the jurisdiction of the school principal. For example, boards of education carry out duties such as maintaining school facilities, managing student attendance, and formulating curriculum policies in accordance with the laws and ordinances. Schools, on the other hand, determine and execute various matters in accordance with procedures set forth in laws, ordinances, and board of education regulations. These matters include student health checks, organization of the school's curriculum including class timetables, and the allocation of duties within the school.

(2) Scope of school management

While the general administration of public schools is the responsibility of boards of education, public schools are required to autonomously develop creative educational activities as dedicated educational institutions that engage directly with students under a period of development.

School management consists of two types of activities: 1) educational activities, which directly engage with students, and 2) administrative activities, which support the cycle of educational activities. The core part of educational activities is organizing, implementing, and evaluating the curriculum, which is performed at an individual school level. Administrative activities, on the other hand, refer to the work of preparing optimal conditions for education, including with respect to personnel, physical facilities and finances. School management can thus be defined as the work of integrating these two sets of activities - educational activities and administrative activities - while strengthening social relations between all interested parties involved in the school with the aim of effectively carrying out the school's educational goals.

(3) Reforming the system of educational administration and school management

In its postwar period, Japan developed a form of educational administration that distributes roles and responsibilities between central and local governments in accordance with the principle of local autonomy. Based on this system, Japan has aimed to equalize educational opportunities and maintain or improve education standards across the country. However, there were also concerns about the operation of this system. Critics argued that the autonomous and innovative efforts of local governments and schools were being hindered by excessive regulation and interference from central and prefectural authorities.

During the 1990s, the government was becoming increasing aware of social change and the need for a policy shift toward competency-based education. A number of national government councils announced that they would promote creative and innovative education at a local level by loosening regulations and allowing local governments and schools to have greater discretion in school education. This policy forms a part of the national-level educational reform package that the government has pursued since 2000. However, progress here has by no means been smooth. The reform of developing discretionary authority over monetary and personnel matters in particular has, as critics point out, stalled across the nation. On the other hand, the expansion of discretions on curriculum and instruction have proceeded to an extent, though a lot of school staff find it difficult to utilize discretions and develop creative activities because of their feeling of limited resources and/or time, deficiency of management skills, and increasing tasks of the school.

2. Organizational Structure of School Management
(1) Intra-school organizational structure

The staffing of schools is provided for primarily in the SEL. Primary and lower secondary schools are required to have the following offices: principal, vice-principal, teacher, nursing teacher, and various clerical staff. In addition to these mandatory posts, schools have the option to deploy a senior vice-principal, senior management teacher, senior advising teacher, diet and nutrition teacher, school dietician, and various other essential staff (see also Part 1, Chapter 4).

a. Principal

The principal is the highest ranking officer in a school. A principal works with the school founder to supervise the duties of all school staff. The SEL defines the principal's duties as being to "govern school management duties and supervise the duties of the school staff." "School management duties" can refer to a wide range of operations, including implementing the school's educational activities, managing school staff, managing students, and managing school facilities. Recent school reforms have further extended the principal's discretionary authority. Principals are now expected to exert instructional leadership and promote "distinctive activities," through formulating a meaningful mission or vision for their school, accelerating organizational learning of teaching staff, and ensuring collaboration with parents and local residents.

b. Staff meetings

An organization that plays an important role in the running of schools in Japan are "staff meetings," a regularly held meeting in which almost all school staff participate. Despite the fact that most schools have routinely held staff meetings since before the post-war era, there were no explicit stipulations on staff meetings in national-level law for many years. This situation led to an intense debate over the nature of staff meetings. The debate centered on the question of whether or not they have decision-making authority. However, under the amendment in 2000, the Ordinance for Enforcement of the SEL defined staff meetings as an "auxiliary body to the principal (not endowed with decision-making authority)," functional for sharing information between staff on school policies and plans, and exchanging opinions.

Pic.3-1 Staff Meeting

(Organized by a principal and usually carried out in the teachers' room)

c. Organization system for allocating school management duties

"School Management Duties," are generally allocated among all school staff under the supervision of the principal. School management duties are generally allocated in two organizational frameworks, educational and administrative. Educational organization defines which teachers are responsible for which academic grades or classes. Administrative organization concerns curriculum affairs, student counselling, health and welfare, and clerical matters. Under this framework, schools establish sections and committees and designate to them responsibility over such administrative matters according to the school's particular circumstances. Generally, each teacher takes on multiple responsibilities in both educational and administrative categories.

Fig. 3-1 Organization of School Management (A Case of Lower Secondary School)

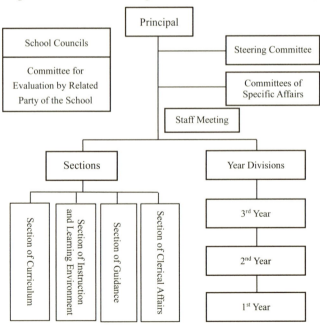

(Source: Prepared by author)

The position of "head teacher" is one that instructs and advises on liaison and coordination, and gives guidance and advice on specific school operations under the supervision of the principal. For instance, primary schools are required to have head teachers on curriculum affairs, affairs of each grade, health affairs. They are also required to have a chief clerk on clerical affairs. These head teachers are assigned in accordance with the relevant school's organizational system for specified school management duties. However, under the current legislation, teachers/senior advising teachers serve as head teachers on an ex officio basis and they are assigned to this position. In other words, head teachers do not have the characteristics of middle-managers and the scope of their duties does not include issuing official orders to other teachers. It should be noted that schools that arrange for senior management teachers to handle specific school operations do not have to assign a head teacher to these duties.

d. Ongoing efforts to rearrange intra-school organization

Traditionally, schools in Japan have adopted a flat organizational structure, with teaching staff other than the principal and vice-principal sharing the same rank. Accordingly, schools' organization has been characterized as a "loosely coupled system" of teachers, each of whom is responsible for a wide variety of duties and has extensive discretionary powers. Hence, many recent researches have highlighted Japanese teachers' heavy workload as an issue. (OECD 2014) [11]

The educational reforms from 2000 onward reflect the intention of MEXT to resolve issues associated with the increasingly diverse and complex workplace that teachers face and rationalize teachers' workload. To this end, the reforms are designed to rearrange intra-school organizational structure based on two

---

11   OECD (2014) *TALIS 2013 Results: An International Perspective on Teaching and Learning*, OECD Publishing.

approaches. The first approach is to strengthen the leadership of principals and establish a vertical command structure in schools by institutionalizing the new posts of vice-principal and senior management teacher as managerial staff supporting the principal. The second approach is to promote horizontal role allocation and coordination by deploying a diet and nutrition teacher and other psychological/ welfare specialists. The 2015 report of the Central Education Council recommended realizing "school as a team" that the government strengthen coordination between teachers and specialist staff, such measures being necessary to improve student counselling and special needs education and to deal effectively with the problems associated with students from disadvantaged families.

(2) School-community interface

Traditionally, for many years Japan lacked an official system for local communities to participate in school management. However, for example, the 2000 Revised Ordinance for Enforcement of the SEL established the position of "school councils". Also, the 2004 Revised LCOOLEA provided a "School Management Council System" enabling schools designated by school founders to have School Management Councils with a certain degree of authority over school management. No.4 of this section will provide a detailed explanation.

3. The Process of School Management
(1) School management cycle

A core part of school management is to optimally utilize the school's conditions and resources while pursuing a continuous cycle of improvements so as to generate positive organizational outcomes and achieve educational objectives. This process is often called the management cycle, and many Japanese schools have applied a PDCA cycle.

The PDCA cycle defines four steps of school management: establishing goals and processing (plan), implementing the plan (do), monitoring activities and outcomes (check), and taking suitable action subsequently (act). Based on this model, many schools formulate an annual plan at the start of each fiscal year in light of their educational/management objectives. The annual plan sets out the school's policies for that year regarding the curriculum, allocation of school duties, staff development, and other matters. The schools then link their annual plan with the teachers' grade/classroom management plans and broadly publicize it in the school directory and other media. At the end of the fiscal year, the principal and the teaching staff assess the extent to which the school achieved its annual plan and identify areas to reinforce in the subsequent fiscal year.

(2) Change in school evaluation

Since 2000, the government has pursued a program of educational administration reform aimed at loosening regulations and extending schools' discretions. On the other hand, MEXT and the boards of education have developed policies for strengthening the "check-act" phase of the PDCA cycle. The motive for this change is a concern over the past management style. Namely, since school management traditionally has a strong tendency to focus on a single year, end of year evaluations of educational and managerial activities are often superficial, meaning that these evaluations often do not lead to improvements in the subsequent fiscal year.

In the Standards for Establishment of Primary/Secondary Schools of 2002 and so forth, MEXT stipulated that schools must make efforts to conduct "self-evaluations" and to publicize their results. School evaluation became a legal requirement with the passing of the 2007 Revised SEL and the Revised Ordinance for Enforcement of the SEL. This legislation mandates that schools be subject to two types of school evaluation: "self-evaluation," to be performed by the school's teachers, and "related-party evaluation," to be conducted by parents and local residents of each school.

In the work carried out by boards of education and schools under this new legal framework, priority is given to the following two tasks: 1) ensuring that the analysis and evaluation of the school's strengths and weaknesses leads to specific remedial actions, and 2) being accountable to parents and local residents for the outcomes of school management and thus establishing a relationship of trust.

4. New Relationship between Schools, Local Communities and Parents
(1) Schools open to the community

At the end of this section, some remarks are put forward on new relationships being formed between Japanese schools, local communities and parents by integrating contemporary educational reform.

Management of schools in Japan has traditionally been strongly standardized due to the relatively strong effects of regulation by MEXT and boards of education. This led to criticism that these schools failed to accommodate various immediate issues in education and a diversity of needs. Since 1990, there has been a growing need for developing unique schools through increased discretionary powers granted to these institutions, and one proposal for a new style of schooling is the idea of "schools open to the communities." An emblematic description of "schools open to the community" can be found in the 1996 report of the Central Council for Education (CCE) "Japanese Education for the 21st Century", which incorporates the aims of: 1) publicizing the state of educational activities to parents and local residents and obtaining feedback from them; 2) actively incorporating support from local households and the community, such as having local people act as part-time teaching staff and volunteers; and 3) providing open, accessible schools and opportunities for learning to residents of the local region and acting as a hub for local activity. Pursuant to this vision, core systems that would fundamentally change the relationship between schools, parents and the local community have been created, such as pursuing open access to school information and creating systems whereby parents and the local community participate in the operation of schools.

(2) School Council

The 1998 report of the CCE "Local Education Administration to Future" proposes that schools ascertain the intentions of parents and local people and reflect these findings into programming in order to promote more open schools in these regions and, in addition, obtain the collaboration of these local stakeholders in operating the schools themselves. To this end, regulatory reform of the Ordinance for Enforcement of the SEL in 2000 established the School Council system. School Councils are installed at each school at the stipulation of the school founder and can provide opinions on the operation of the school as requested by the principal. The School Council is composed of non-faculty members with expertise and understanding of education, recommended by the principal, with the founder of the school entrusting the council with said duties. Approximately 80% of public schools nationwide have School Councils and, while they legally do not maintain assembly conference capacity, they host meetings at which opinions are sought in 95% of schools.

(3) School Management Council

Since its inception, the School Council system has been criticized for being merely a formality due to the fact that its provision of opinions is only done at the request of the principal and that the council is not granted specific authority. The LCOOLEA were revised in 2004, and the School Management Council system was adopted. Through this council, which operates under a parliamentary system, parents and members of the local community are guaranteed certain rights that allow them to take part in the operation of schools. Schools that have a School Management Council are referred to as "Community Schools." School Management Councils are granted the right to: 1) approve a basic policy for operation of the school; 2) provide opinions to the board of education and principal regarding operation of the school; and 3) provide opinions to those persons with appointive power over hiring of faculty. As of April 1st, 2017, the numbers of community schools were 3,600 and were increasing mainly throughout primary, lower and upper secondary schools.

Compared to the School Council System, the School Management Council System allows for local community members and parents to actively partake in the operation of schools.

Surveys of specific principals have found that community schools have succeeded in: 1) allowing schools and local communities to share information with each other; 2) making local communities collaborate with schools; and 3) fostering the creation of unique schools. [12] When the system was first launched, emphasis was put on the School Management Council's role as a means of ushering in changes in governance towards reform of school operations through participation by local peoples and parents. Regarding this fact, however, it is mostly employed as a means of promoting support of schools by the local community. As schools are increasingly called on to accommodate the growing complexity of issues faced by children and for schools, the community, and households to collaborate together in the growth of children, community schools are being sought as a tool used to promote a shift towards "schools that co-exist with the community." The law was amended again in April 2017, with the role of the School Management Council defined as supporting school operations, and with language, compelling schools to make efforts to install these councils. Going forward, schools will be called on to treat the local community as a partner in creating a scholastic system for social education that will allow for mutually support of children's social and academic growth.

(4) Parental involvement
a. Classroom observation

Several times a year, classes are opened up for observation by parents.

---

12   Sato, H.et al. (2010) *The Study of Community Schools* (in Japanese), Kazamashobo, p.112

Generally a one-hour lesson for each academic grade is made public, and parents visit the classroom to observe. In recent years, some schools have launched "open school" programs, whereby the schools are open from the start of classes through to the end of the school day, with visitors permitted to come and go freely. In addition to the courses themselves, break time, lunches, and other day-to-day activities are also made public. After these classroom observations, there are also opportunities for teachers and parents to discuss and engage, fostering mutual understanding between the school and parents and engendering deeper collaboration.

b. PTA

In many schools, a formalized Parent Teacher Association (PTA) exists. However, there are still many cases that have not succeeded in fostering active participation or where there are no suitable candidates to serve as PTA members, causing the PTA to be perfunctory or exist only in its name. A recent issue drawing attention is that some PTAs effectively employ compulsory participation.

With the aforementioned School Management Council, council members form part of the PTA by acting as representatives for parents. However, the council itself is largely composed of local residents, so its meetings tend to under-represent comments by young parents. In order for the PTA to remain pertinent, changes must be made in order to allow the opinions of these parents to be reflected in the management of schools

Chapter 4. Teacher System

1. The Position of Teachers and Other School Personnel in Public Education

(1) The basic characteristics of the teaching profession

In the Fundamental Law of Education (enacted in 1947), Article 6 set out provisions for schools and teachers. Paragraph 1 requires that school education be "public nature." From that, Paragraph 2 stipulates that the teachers in charge of school education of this nature shall be "servants of the whole community" be aware of their mission, and strive to discharge their duties. It goes on to say that, for teachers to discharge their mission and duties, their status shall be respected and their fair and appropriate treatment shall be ensured.

In the 2006 revisions to the law, however, the substance of Paragraph 2 concerning teachers was set out independently as "Article 9 (Teachers)," as follows:

Teachers of the schools prescribed by law shall endeavor to fulfill their duties, while being deeply conscious of their noble mission and continuously devoting themselves to research and self-cultivation. (2) Considering the importance of the mission and duties of the teachers set forth in the preceding paragraph, the status of teachers shall be respected, their fair and appropriate treatment ensured, and measures shall be taken to improve their education and training.

Although the revised act adopts some wording from the old act, the phrase "Teachers of the schools . . . shall be servants of the whole community" has been deleted, and the words "noble" and "deeply" have been added to "conscious of their mission." In addition, "continuously devoting themselves to research and self-cultivation" has been inserted to Paragraph 1, and "improve their education and training" to Paragraph 2.

Nevertheless, as stipulated in Paragraph 1 of Article 6 of the new act, they maintain that school education be "public nature," so the public nature of the duties of teachers has not changed.

On the aim of education, the revised act states, "Education shall aim for the full development of personality and strive to nurture citizens, sound in mind and body, who are imbued with the qualities necessary to form a peaceful and democratic state and society." The professional duties and responsibilities of the teachers tasked with achieving this aim have special characteristics that make them different from those of employees in general public services. Given these special characteristics, both the new and old acts stipulate that, for teachers to fulfill their professional responsibilities, their status must be respected at both societal and institutional levels and that their fair and appropriate treatment must be ensured. Let us look at how these are guaranteed in terms of actual institutions.

(2) The status and treatment of teachers

Teachers at public schools possess the status of local public service employees, and as such the Local Public Service Act applies to them. Yet based on the special characteristics of their duties and responsibilities, a special law called the Special Act for Education Personnel is applied and steps are taken that are different from those of general public service employees. For teachers at private schools, because they are employees of those schools, work regulations—which are drafted by the individual legally-incorporated educational institution—in line with the Labor Standards Act, the Labor Union Act, and similar laws are applied. With the incorporation of national universities in 2004, the status of teachers at national schools became that of employees of national university corporations, and the work regulations of the individual national university corporation are applied.

"Fair and appropriate treatment" refers to proper and just treatment in terms of status and salary. To secure qualified teacher personnel and to maintain or otherwise improve the quality of education, the Act on Special Measures concerning Assurance of Educational Personnel for Compulsory Education

Schools for Purpose of Maintenance and Improvement of School Education Standards was promulgated. It lays out provisions by which salaries that are preferential compared to salary standards of general public services employees are given to teachers. In addition, Article 13 of the Law for Special Regulations concerning Educational Public Service Personnel stipulates that the salaries of teachers at public schools can be established based on the special characteristics of their duties and responsibilities. Non-administrative teaching personnel at public schools are exempted from the provisions concerning augmented wages for overtime work that are set out in Article 37 of the Labor Standards Act, which means that they do not receive overtime pay that commensurates with the amount of overtime hours worked. Instead, they receive "teaching profession adjustments," which are fixed at 4 percent of salaries for all teachers.

Teachers and other personnel at municipal schools whose wages are paid by the prefecture in which they are located are referred to as "prefecture funded school personnel." Based on the principle that the establishing organization should defray expenses, the salaries of these should, as a general rule, be paid by the municipalities that set these schools up, but in some cases special measures such as these are taken to prevent disparities in education standards from arising as a result of a municipality's financial capabilities. It is also worthy of note that every year there are major transfers of personnel among public schools. This is one of the distinguishing features of Japan's employment system for teachers. These personnel transfers take place for the purpose of: 1) contributing to the improvement of the makeup of organizations of teachers at individual schools, 2) eliminating disparities among schools and regions, and 3) encouraging the revitalization of individual schools while raising the quality and capabilities of individual teachers as well as their morale.

(3) Duties of teachers

Educational public employees should obey the following duties as stated in the Local Public Service Law and National Public Service Law: The duties of obeying not only laws and ordinances but also official orders by superior officers / The duties of devoting oneself to one's given work / The prohibition of acts of losing reliance / The duties of maintaining secrecy obtained during one's work / The limitation of political activities / The prohibition of labor disputes / The limitations on engaging in a profit-making enterprise.

(4) Types of teachers and other school personnel and their job descriptions

Teachers and other school personnel in Japan are divided into many job types depending on job descriptions. Schools have principals, deputy vice-principals, teachers, nurse-teachers, and clerks. Principals manage school affairs and direct the personnel. Deputy vice-principals help the principal, arrange school affairs, and educate students if necessary. Teachers are responsible for student education. Nurse-teachers are in charge of student nurses. Clerks manage school clerical work. Due to revisions to the School Education Law in 2005, food and nutrition teachers were established and revisions in 2007 included vice-principals, senior teachers, and chief supervising teachers. In recent years, reforms have been pushed forward for the purpose of improving the organizational management and leadership frameworks that would allow for schools to be managed in a more systematic and dynamic manner under the leadership of school principals.

2. Pre-Service Training, Employment, and In-Service Training of Teachers, and an Overview of Systems
(1) The principle of "teacher training in colleges and universities" and the principle of an "open system"

The system of teacher training in present-day Japan is based on the principle of "teacher training in colleges and universities" and the principle of an "open system." The former aims for the training of teachers as professionals who have acquired specialized, scientific knowledge concerning education, including specialized academic knowledge about academia, the sciences, and the arts, as well as the principles of child development and the logic of school subjects rooted in character building through research and education at college or university. The latter seeks to secure a broad base of human resources with diverse personalities and skills by making teacher training possible at a wide range of colleges and universities, rather than establishing specific institutions for teacher training.

These two major philosophies are based on reexaminations of the way the pre-war teacher training system worked. To establish a modern system of education, the training of teachers in large numbers was an urgent matter for Japan. The first shihan gakkō, or "normal school," (the precursor to teachers' colleges) in the country was established in Tokyo in September of 1872. By around 1880 there was at least one normal school in each prefecture. This allowed for a systematically planned supply of teachers. After this, Japan then shifted its focus to the training of teachers who could meet the expectations of the state. A type of teacher referred to as the "shihan-type" subsequently arose in the national consciousness, and the closed nature of this system came to be seen as problematic. In the post-war years, when the new school system was established, a new principle for teacher training that met the needs of the new system came into being.

(2) Credentialism, types of certificates, and their validity

The stated purpose of the Education Personnel Certification Act is to "prescribe standards concerning the certification of educational personnel and to maintain and improve the quality of educational personnel." The reigning principle governing the qualifications for educational personnel is "credentialsim." Article 1 of the School Education Law stipulates that the positions of senior teacher, chief supervising teacher, teacher, assistant teacher, nurse-teacher, assistant nurse-teacher, food and nutrition teacher, instructors at kindergartens, primary schools, lower secondary schools, upper secondary schools, combined upper/lower secondary education schools, and special education schools must have a certificate corresponding to each position outlined in this law.

When the Education Personnel Certification Act was first promulgated, it was hoped that academic fields related to the work of education would sufficiently advance so that education could be nurtured as a dedicated profession that deals with the fostering of people based on academic fundamentals. Credentialism was a basic principle meant to guarantee the level of expertise required of the education profession. However, with the establishment and expansion of the special teacher's certificate system and special part-time teacher's certificate system that resulted from revisions to the Education Personnel Certification Act that took place from 1988 to 1998, and with revision of the Ministry Ordinance for Enforcement of the School Education Law from 2001 to 2006 that made it possible to appoint principals and vice principals who do not have teaching certificates, there was no choice but to revise the principle of credentialism.

There are three classifications of certificates: regular, special, and temporary. Regular teaching certificates are granted to those persons who has completed the required credits at a college, university or designated training institution, or to those persons who have passed an educational personnel exam. This regular teaching certificate is valid in all prefectures, but due to revisions to the Education Personnel Certification Act made in 2007, it is only valid for 10 years from the day after it was granted to the last day of the academic year in which 10 years have passed. There are three divisions of regular certificate classification: regular schoolteacher, nurse teacher, and food and nutrition teacher. Certificates are divided into three classifications depending on the highest level of education completed and the type of credits he/she obtained. Those who have successfully completed graduate school and have received a Master's degree qualify for an advanced certificate, those with a Bachelor's degree receive a first class certificate, and those with an Associate's degree, junior college graduates, receive a second class certificate.

Special certificates are awarded to those who have specialized knowledge or skills, and are valid for no more than 10 years within the prefecture which issued them while regular certificates are nationally recognized and have no expiry date. Temporary certificates are issued to assistant teachers, only when teachers with regular certificates are difficult to recruit, and are valid for three years within the issuing prefecture.

(3) An overview of teacher employment and in-service training systems

Whereas the employment and promotion of general public service employees are based on competitive examinations, the employment of teachers for public schools is done via "screening." This screening is undertaken by the superintendent of education at the prefectural board of education who has appointive power. "Screening" is defined as "determinations made by an appointer who is deemed qualified—by virtue of background, expertise, or qualification—to make said determinations as to whether, based on compliance with criteria established by that appointer, a person possesses the required ability and aptitude for a government post."

"Training" entails research and self-cultivation, and unlike general public service employees whose training is for the purpose of "developing and improving work efficiency", educational public service employees undergo training that is mandated by the special characteristics of their professional duties and responsibilities. This is based on the acknowledgment that research predicated on educational activities, and self-cultivation to improve one's character—insofar that the purpose of education is to fully develop the human character—are requisites in education.

If we look at training in terms of how it is handled as a part of public service duties, it can be divided into three types: 1) training assigned as an order issued in the course of duties, 2) training ordered due to exemptions from duties of devotion to service, and 3) voluntary training received outside of work hours.

Examples are: Self-training, School-based training, Training by various organizations, Training offered by the authorities of educational administration, and Training at universities. Furthermore, training can be categorized depending on the place in which it is given. There are systematic improvements being pursued in many places in Japan to make it easier for teachers to get training that accommodates individual stages in teachers' lives, i.e. training administered at the right timing in their professional lives and that encompasses content and methods suited to their age and level of experience. Content-wise, training can be categorized as: 1) training for new employs, 2) training conducted according to teaching experience (training for teachers with 5, 10, and 20 years experience), and 3) training tailored to professional rank and/or field of specialty (training for leading support teachers, newly appointed head of school affairs, vice principals, and pro vice-principals).

Systems for teacher training have been expanded for the purpose of improving the quality of teaching. The initial training system was established in the 1989 academic year. In this system, teacher candidates undergo in-school and out-of-school training based on the instruction and advice of their chief supervising teacher while working as probationary teachers for a period of one year. When this training period is over, the school principal evaluates the job performance of the candidate based on his or her attitude toward training and performance of practical educational duties, and then decides on whether to employ the candidate as a full-time teacher. The probationary employment period for general local public service employees is six months, but due to the specialized nature of the professional duties of teachers this has been extended to one year. Moreover, the 2003 academic year saw the implementation of training for teachers with 10 years of experience. Also of note is that in the 2001 academic year a work leave/sabbatical system for graduate students was established for the purpose of expanding opportunities for teachers to enroll in domestic or overseas graduate programs and earn certifications. Furthermore in 2008, graduate schools of teacher education were established with the hope of nuturing mid-level teachers who will play a central role in improving school systems.

Pic. 4-1 In-service Training for New Principals

(conducted to new principals of primary schools by a board of education)

3. Reforms Involving the Quality of Teachers and Other School Personnel and Changes in the Environments that Teachers Face

In Japan, the view of teachers cultivated since the Meiji Period as members of a "holy profession" and the post-war view, spurred on chiefly by the labor union movement, of teachers as "laborers in the field of education" have been in conflict. The ILO/UNESCO "Recommendation concerning the Status of Teachers" held that "Teaching should be regarded as a profession" and similar views of education as a specialized profession quickly took hold. Nevertheless, the actual substance of views of education as a specialized profession is not always readily clear. In fact, in reports of official deliberation held over the years, it has been common to describe the ideal teacher by merely reciting lists of qualities and abilities that they should possess. In this process, the points of emphasis for teachers have shifted from a broad, rich academic and cultural education to a sense of mission and practical instructional skills.

In a 1987 report by the Teacher Training Council titled "Measures to Improve the Qualities and Abilities of Teachers" the capabilities of teachers are referred to by the term "practical instructional skills." The document goes on to define the fundamentals as "a deep understanding of the sense of mission as educators and of the growth and development of humans, an affection towards infants, young pupils and students, specialized knowledge of subjects taught, and a broad and rich academic and cultural education." It also states that the qualities and abilities of a teacher are molded through each stage of pre-service training, employment, and in-service training, and that measures to enhance them must comprehensively address each of these stages. Based on this, the report suggested policies for concrete improvements, which were codified in the 1988 revisions of the Education Personnel Certification Act.

In its 1997 report stated "As for qualities and abilities that will be particularly required of teachers in the future, the most important will be the ability to nurture in children the 'ability to live' regardless of turbulent times.".

(1) The increasing stringency of personnel management

In spite of implementing a range of measures, the problematic situation has not seen much progress and as a consequence, doubts have grown about the fundamental qualities required of teachers. In 2001, a system for designating teachers as "deficient in instructional skills" was instituted. This lead to the nation-wide implementation of the New Teacher Evaluation System. Article 47 (2) of the Act on the Organization and Operation of Local Educational Administration stipulates that those persons whose ability to instruct young pupils or students is deficient, and who have shown no effective improvement despite training or other measures to remedy this deficiency, shall be relieved of their duties. This makes it is possible to employ them as full-time employees of the relevant prefecture for positions other than teaching. The determination of whether a teacher is "deficient in instructional skills" ultimately falls to the board of education of the relevant prefecture. In another noteworthy development, the teaching certificate renewal system, which had already been proposed as an idea in a Central Council for Education (CCE) report titled "Ideals for the Future of the Education Personnel Certification System," was adopted in 2008.

(2) The trend toward operational improvements in schools

Meanwhile, as the issues schools face become increasingly diverse, complex, and difficult, it has become clear that more and more teachers are working exceedingly long hours. According to a survey investigating the realities of the work of teachers done by the Ministry of Education, Culture, Sports, Science and Technology in 2006, the average number of overtime hours worked per month, including work days and off days, amounted to about 42 hours. Compared to a 1966 survey looking at the same factors, this amounts to a roughly five-fold increase. According to results published in 2014 by the OECD Teaching and Learning International Survey, lower secondary school teachers worked an average of 53.9 hours per week, which was the highest among all countries that participated in the survey (38.3 hours per week was the average for countries that joined the survey). Of particular note was the 7.7 hours spent coaching extracurricular activities (compared to 2.1 hours) and the 5.5 hours (compared to 2.9 hours) doing administrative paperwork. These figures clearly show that teachers' time spent outside scheduled teaching duties is on the rise.

Teachers today must be able to adapt to reforms to educational curricula and classroom methods, as well as to new challenges such as English, morals, ICT, and special-needs education. Moreover, schools themselves are changing in major ways, moving increasingly toward the concept of "schools as teams." Amid these changes, there are efforts currently underway to "rationalize" work in schools so that the teachers can concentrate on the teaching of topics and the guidance of their students, which constitute the professional duties that they were hired to perform in the first place. Reforms are already underway to instill the notion of the "ever-learning teacher". These reforms that are rooted in the Central Council for Education report titled "The Enhancement of Qualities and Capabilities of Teachers Responsible for the Future of School Education: Toward the Creation of Mutual Learning and Mutual Developing Teacher Training Communities."

Pic.4-2 Lesson Study

(Many teachers from other schools observing a physical education class. Afterwards, teachers discuss ways to improve the teaching method)

Column-6: Lesson Study

Lesson study is a process to improve teaching skills with one's colleagues through observation. This system has been succeeded since 1872, and consisted of three steps, examining teaching material, observing actual class lessons, and discussion afterwards.

As curriculum guidelines are provided by the central government, teaching skills as well as classroom management became the major topic among teachers and this climate has become a tradition gradually.

This unique atmosphere is known as Lesson study, and in 1999, a comparison of math classes between Japan and the U.S. revealed, "Lesson study largely contributed to the success of Japanese classes." This recognition led to the term "Lesson study" becoming well known around the world.

Japanese Lesson study skill has been widely incorporated. Teachers from the same or different schools can discuss teaching materials and creating lesson guides for children. Lessons can also be compared on-site. Moreover, board of education superintendents and outside teachers are invited to the meetings where all the participants can improve their teaching skills. This rather unique method is the result of its format. The scope in which Lesson Study is implemented varies by organization, but the most effective one is "in-school training". Theme setting, lesson planning and its implementation, post-lesson meetings, research bulletins, and other cooperative activities improve the teaching ability of each teacher and the overall teamwork of the entire school. This system is often said to be constructed of professional learning communities.

However, Lesson study has the problem of less opportunity, reduced number of leaders, and newly appointed teachers in recent years. In order to solve such issues, the leaders are expected to plan and organize Lesson Study activities to contribute to raising not only the teaching quality, but students' achievement and hence, make the atmosphere of school more active and attractive as a whole.

Chapter 5. Private Schools

1. Definition of Private School

Private schools are those established by an incorporated educational institution (IEI). An "incorporated educational institution" means a juridical body formed for the purpose of establishing a private school, which is one of the entities authorized as school establishing body by the Fundamental Law of Education (FLE) and the School Education Law (SEL) As for kindergartens, those provided by individuals, religious corporations, or social welfare corporations are deemed as private schools as well, since kindergartens are not required to be established by only incorporated educational institutions. In addition to these schools, schools established by business corporations and non-profit organizations, for which the New Structural Reform Special District Law offers an exception to the SEL, are also regarded as "private schools".

Before World War II, school education was authorized exclusively by the state, and private schools were considered to be ancillary to public schools. In the current legal framework, they are positioned as schools "bearing a certain responsibility for education, in other words, as "a part of education system which guarantees the fundamental right to education" along with public schools. This situation can be called private schools with public nature. The term "schools" or "schools prescribed by law" used in educational laws includes not only public schools, but also private schools, which means private schools are subject to the applicable laws. They are required to meet the necessary standards for school facilities, class composition, curriculum, and so on.

On the other hand, each private school is established by donations from private individuals and provides a unique education based on educational philosophies, values and views on humanity or religious principles, expressed in its spirit of foundation. This feature is usually called the autonomy of private schools. In order to promote their autonomy and uniqueness, administrative intervention for private schools is limited. The public nature and autonomy of private schools are put in a statutory form in a new article in the FLE revised in 2006.

Thus, private schools carry missions different from those of public schools to ensure public benefit, stability, and consistency as public education while exerting autonomy and distinctiveness as private education organizations. For their management, a different institutionalized mechanism is implemented so that both features can be balanced.

2. General Features
(1) Current situation of private schools
a. The number of private schools and enrollment

The numbers and enrollment of private schools for each category of school establishing body is shown at the end of the book. Although only 10% of primary and lower secondary schools are private, private schools account for 30% of upper secondary schools and more than 80% of higher education institutions. In regard to enrollment, as much as 80% of university students, 30% of upper secondary students and 80% of kindergarteners are enrolled in the private sector. Thus, private schools have been playing a significant role in Japanese public education. Over the last 10 years, the number of private schools at the compulsory education stage has been increasing. Also, co-education is the norm in publicly provided schools, but it is a distinguishing point among private schools that nearly 30% of them are single-sex schools after primary education.

Tuition is not required for public school which the Constitution and FLE stipulate, but in the case of private school, tuition fee etc. is required. The amount differs by stage of education, location, size, school policy, and so on.

Teachers in private schools are required to have a teaching certificate or other qualification to be employed like those of public schools, but their working conditions are slightly different according to the school policy, its financial situation, etc.

b. Geographical distribution

Private schools are concentrated in urban areas for every educational stage in general. It is especially notable in higher education. The top three prefectures in school number (Tokyo, Osaka, Aichi) combine for 33% of all junior colleges and universities, and in enrollment (Tokyo, Osaka, Kanagawa) for 40% in higher education.

c. Religions of private schools

About one fourth of private schools are religious schools founded on religious beliefs. Their percentage increases with descending school level to as much as 47% for primary schools. 67% of religious schools are Christian, and Buddhist schools make up the second most.

(2) Primary and secondary private school

Curriculum should be organized according to the SEL and national standard even in private schools. However, the course of study is a general standard and some space is left to be prepared by individual schools. In this way, private schools are able to make efforts to highlight their features as much as possible in particular, length of academic term, school holidays and number of classes in a week.

The FLE prohibits specific religious education and activities in any public school and must provide a secular education. However, such education and activities are permitted in private schools and religious studies can replace subjects of morality.

So many private schools have multiple schools at different stages of education at the same time and some of them have continuity from kindergarten to university. Thus continuous education is a particular feature of them.

3. The Organization and Management of Incorporated Educational Institutions (IEI)

IEI is managed by a board of directors comprised of five or more directors, one of whom is appointed as a president. Besides the board, an IEI has two or more auditors to evaluate performance including accounting. The usual business is determined according to the board's decisions concerning its policy and budget.

An IEI should have a board of councilors consisting of employees and graduates in order to reflect their opinions on its management. The president must listen to their opinions regarding important matters such as budgets and borrowings, disposition of important assets, business plans, revision of the articles of endowment, mergers and dissolution, etc.

To ensure a fair and reasonable operation of an IEI, family members or relatives are prohibited from composing particular staff.

4. The Competent Authorities and Autonomy of Private Schools

The Private Schools Act stipulates the competent administrative authorities according to the type of private school as shown in **Table 5-1**.

Although such authorities may request a private school to submit reports as to curriculum, school finances and management when necessary, they have no power to intervene except in a case of emergency.

Table 5-1 The Competent Authorities

competent authorities	targets
MEXT	Provide and maintain higher education institutions & any other schools at the same time
Prefectural governor	Other private schools apart from upper column
Head of a municipality	Integrated early childhood education and care center located in a designated city or a core city

Thus, the reason why power of competent authorities is restricted to a minimum is to maintain respect for the autonomy of private schools as much as possible and to ensure the development of private schools.

While administrative power is restricted, private school councils are provided in the prefecture as an advisory organization to the competent authority. It consists of 10 to 20 members appointed by the governor from among persons with relevant knowledge and experience in education, such as the principals of the private schools, the presidents of IEIs, education experts, and former educational administrators. The opinions and recommendations put forth should be from a professional point of view and in advance of making influential decisions.

5. Legal Structure for Private Schools
(1) Private Schools Act

The private school system is regulated by two kinds of regulations, firstly, FLE and secondly, the specified registration for education. The Private Schools Act (1949), the Act on Subsidies for Private Schools and the Accounting Standard for Incorporated educational Institutions belong to the latter which is applied only to private schools.

The FLE affirms all schools are public nature. Hence, to respect the autonomy of private schools and on the basis of these laws, the Private Schools Act was enacted for the purpose of promoting their sound progress. It clearly reduced the administrative power to control private schools, and introduced three principles to promote education within them. Firstly, it emphasized their autonomy, and secondly, it stipulated original power and duty as to the organizing/dissolving of IEI, and also managing polity and its actual business to realize the public nature of private schools. Finally, it provides institutional foundations for subsidies from public funds.

(2) Act on Subsidies for Private Schools and Accounting Standards for IEIs

As private schools are regarded as a part of formal educational organizations that guarantee children's rights to education, they are required to be firmly managed and supply a proper education. Continuous well-balanced financial management is most important for the IEI. At the same time, school expenses which parents have to pay should be mitigated based on the actual situation of students' household. From this context, The Private Schools Act authorizes subsidies from the central and prefectural governments to IEIs to help private schools flourish. Also, the Act on Subsidies for Private Schools systemizes the basic rules for the subsidies and simultaneously stipulates a provision for supervision by the competent authorities in association with financial assistance.

The Act on Subsidies for Private Schools requires that the IEI which receives ordinary expense subsidies should follow the fixed account process and prepare financial documents attached to an audit report in accordance with the Accounting Standard for IEI which is applicable only to them, and submited to the competent authorities.

6. Promotion of Private Schools: the Efficacy and the Problems

FLE clearly stipulates that the central and local governments shall endeavor to promote private school education through subsidies and other appropriate means and in this way, such a subsidy system has been developed. Although this system has brought a kind of benefit to private schools and its managing board by giving them a certain monetary amount from public authorities. However, private schools are obliged to submit to regulation inspections and other rules. It should be noted that private schools are under the control of public authorities as they constitute a part of formal education that is subsidized from public funds.

(1) Autonomy and control

As stated above, sources of a private school's revenue come from not only their own resources, but also from ordinary expense subsidies from the government. The financial assistance from public funds can be justified on the basis that private school education contributes to public interests, and hence the public nature of private schools.

However, Article 89 of the Constitution of Japan prohibits public expenditure to any charitable, educational or benevolent enterprises without control of public authority. In this context, such conflict between the control of public authority and autonomy of private schools can be easily recognized and historically, there had been a long controversy whether the subsidies are constitutional or not. If private schools fall under the control of the public authority, the subsidies should be constitutional. On the other hand, such control intervenes or encroaches on their autonomy to develop their own unique and characteristic education. On the contrary, if private schools ask to be free from public control, putting more value on their autonomy, the subsidies are unconstitutional and they will lose those financial benefits.

The introduction of the Act on Subsidies for Private Schools in 1975 gave a legal foundation to the subsidies. It clearly showed the principle and basic policies for funding, and also recognized the original and significant role that private schools fulfill in Japanese school system. On the other hand, competent authorities were vested with the power to affirm the performance of private schools.

At present, it is commonly understood that private schools are under the public control for they are asked to comply with regulations on management of IEIs, school facilities, curriculum, teachers' qualifications, and so on. However, as the control is limited as already explained in 3-(1), certain autonomy of private schools is preserved in that it is possible for them to develop unique and characteristic education.

Thus, the most distinctive feature of Japanese private schools is that they usually accept financial assistance from public funds and public control in return.

(2) Problems of subsidies

Tuition and other payments from the students cover about 50% of imputed income of a private school. A dramatic decline in enrollment mirroring the drop in birth rate has caused a considerable reduction in the ratio of enrollment to enrollment quota and tuition income. This situation constitutes a significant factor for the financial instability of private schools. On the other hand, the total amount of subsidies has remained the same for last 10 years. As for universities, the ratio of subsidies to revenue peaked in 1980 and has been diminished to 10%. As for upper secondary schools it's 30%, which is far from sufficient for maintaining healthy finances.

The ordinary expense subsidies consist of two kinds. One is the general subsidies for the salary expenses for teachers and other personnel, and costs of education and research activities. The other one is the special subsidies for the promotion of education and research of specific areas. In recent trends, the policy for the promotion of substantial development in specified fields has brought increased subsidies for those fields and in return, a gradual decrease can be observed in general subsidies, and serious competition for subsidies among private has increased because of this policy. It is of concern that these policies have led to much more public administrative intervention than ever and is misgiven to lose their autonomy and steer them into uniformed education.

In addition, a seriously disproportionate allocation of the subsidies is a key issue for universities, because it could force small or local universities without a firm financial background to close down.

Chapter 6. Social Education

1. Legal Position

Like school education, social education systems are regulated by educational laws including the Constitution. Especially the Social Education Law plays a major role stipulating the duties of the central and local governments concerning social education. The Social Education Law codifies the responsibilities of social education administration in order to secure the freedom of social education as a people's self-education and to develop it on the philosophy of education reform of the post-war period.

(1) Social Education Law

The Social Education Law stipulates that "organizational educational activities (including physical education and recreational activities) are mainly conducted for adolescents and adults except for educational activities conducted as school curriculums". This includes non-formal education such as learning activities at a community learning center and in-service corporate trainings. However, people who left school are subject to social education, but any activities for children outside the school, such as outdoor activities and activities after school, are also regarded as within the scope of social education.

Social education is an organizational educational activity, but its contents and learning methods are diverse. Although individuals learn by themselves, that is not unilateral training. A characteristic of social education is that people learn from each other and have elements of self-education in relation to others. Social education makes up a large part of the concept of lifelong learning. However, lifelong learning includes formal school education, informal education from one's family, and other accidental learning activities which gives it a broader concept than social education.

(2) The Fundamental Law of Education (FLE)

The FLE stipulates the nature of social education and shows the specific ways of encouragement and promotion by central and local governments. Because social education is carried in response to individual requests and social demands (Article 12), much more educational opportunities are encouraged by administrative authorities. In other words, it is necessary for central and local governments to develop an environment that can respond to the diverse learning needs of citizens in a varied society with a broad perspective. The methods of promoting social education are establishing social education facilities, using school facilities, providing learning opportunities and information, cooperation with family education and school education, etc.

2. Social Education Facilities

Central and local governments will provide social education facilities for people for social education activities. The representatives are libraries, museums and community learning centers, and there are also youth education facilities, outdoor activity facilities, social sports or women's education facilities and so on. In recent years, private institutions are responsible for the management of public facilities and the Private Finance Initiative program has been partially introduced. There are some cases where social education facilities are provided as a part of complex facilities with other administrative fields or commercial facilities.

(1) Library

The Library Act prescribes the character of libraries based on the spirit of the Social Education Law. Public libraries provided by local governments are located throughout the country, and the number is increasing slightly.

Library services include collecting and laying out materials, browsing and lending to users, reference services, reading consultation, guidance for use, gatherings such as reading and lecture meetings, etc. Furthermore, emphasis is also placed on mutual lending in cooperation with other libraries, cooperation with schools, and encouraging the utilization of learning outcomes. Libraries are a social educational facility that accumulate materials and information systematically and responds to the learning needs of users and develops educational functions to solve community problems for local people. In order to develop such professional qualities to perform these services, the Library Act stipulates librarian qualifications.

Pic. 6-1 Mobile Library

(A mobile library is usually utilized in areas where the residents feel difficult to access to a library. It has about 3,000 books.)

(2) Museum

The Museum Act also specifies the character of museums based on the "spirit of Social Education Law". Museums are an agency that collect and keep materials, promote education, conduct research and so on. The entrance fee to public museums is free in principle, but unlike libraries, it can be charged if there are unavoidable circumstances for their operation.

Various materials are entrusted to museums, from humanities such as history, art, life, folklore studies, to a wide range of natural systems such as astronomy, science, natural history, and general museums. Since zoos, botanical gardens, aquariums, etc. are included, the variation is really abundant. In recent years, emphasis has been placed on cooperation with schools and encouraging the utilization of learning outcomes. In order to guarantee the qualities of professional staff's activities, the Museum Act stipulates curator qualifications.

(3) Community Learning Center (Kominkan)

Community learning centers, called Kominkan, have been established by municipalities as bases for promoting activities of communities and daily social education. They spread from rural areas to all over the country, and actually stand in every lower secondary school district, but their numbers are decreasing due to recent financial influences. Community learning centers in Japan attract world-wide attention as a model of community based learning centers developed mainly in Asian countries.

Pic. 6-2 One of the Activities of a Community Learning Center (Tea Ceremony)

(One of the popular activities provided by a local learning center. Flower arrangement, computer learning etc. take place as well.)

The function of community learning centers as prescribed by the Social Education Law is "opening a regular course" (Article 22 of the Social Education

Law). It encourages and promotes autonomous social educational activities by implementing various projects, providing facilities for local people, and collaborating with various organizations and institutions. Centers are expected to be free from commercial, political, and religious activities. There is no regulation as to their fees, many municipalities have the "free principle" and are usually run using local expenditure. But for a few municipalities, due to financial difficulties, customers are asked to pay the fee.

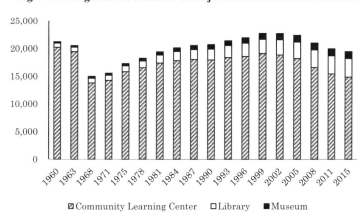

Fig. 6-1 Changes in the Number of Major Social Education Facilities

(MEXT, Social Education Survey)

(4) School facilities for social education

The FLE, the Social Education Law, and the SEL stipulate that school facilities can be used for social education. This was called "open school", and schools were used as a place for social education in times when social education facilities were not properly provided, and their teaching staff also played a certain role in social education activities. However, it is limited to cases where it is deemed that school educational activities are not hindered. In practice, approval must be given by the board of education, and also the board of education must ask the school principal whether it is feasible or not.

3. Social education officials

Social education officials are expected to have certain expertise and leadership roles, but the legal position depends on the type of social education facility. At present, there are differences in placement situation depending on prefectures and municipalities.

(1) Social education supervisor

The social education supervisor is "professional education staff" alongside the supervisor for schools. Their duty is to give professional technical advice and guidance to those who carry out social education. There is no legal hierarchical relationship between the social education supervisor and the social educator regarding command or supervision. The Social Education Law stipulates that a social education supervisor shall be allocated in the administrative office of the board of education of prefectures and municipalities. This system was mandated by municipalities as a result of the amendment of the law in 1959, but from 1974, it was dispatched from prefectures to municipalities, and the prefectural government was responsible for half the salary. Currently expenditure by the central government is abolished, and their numbers have decreased gradually.

(2) Staff of social education facilities

Staffs in facilities concerning social education are involved in their management and operation, and providing information and consultation to people. Although they are expected to perform based on their competence and expertise, their professional positions are not legally sufficient. The social education supervisor may also serve concurrently as a community learning center staff member, and sometimes part-time staff may be employed. Librarians and museum curators have legal grounds as professional staff and require certain qualifications and training, but in the case of social education staff, contents and quality of their duty differ from time to time and place to place, so it is still difficult to raise their status.

(3) Social education board

In a social education committee, members are arbitrarily placed in the prefectural or municipal board of education. The purpose is to incorporate people's needs into social education administration in order to promote social education activities according to local circumstances. When local governments give subsidies to organizations related social education, they must listen to the opinions of the social education board in advance. Although there are differences depending on prefectures and municipalities, it is expected that more active discussion take place to reflect public opinion in policies.

4. Social education administration

For the purpose of social education to be realized at any time and place, central and local governments must arrange a suitable environment in which the citizens can develop their cultural enrichment which may contribute to raise the quality of life.

(1) Role and organization of the state

The state indirectly encourages learners basically through assistance and guidance advice to local governments. As any grants by the state are expended within the range of budget, such grants as well as expenditure for social education have been minimized in recent years. The role of the state is to engage in formulating standards relating to social education facilities and administrative affairs related to training and qualifications of social education staff. In addition, it also implements educational activities on the promotion of social education, give assistance and guidance advice to nationwide social education related organizations, surveys research, etc. The central government is responsible for the Lifelong Learning Policy Bureau of the MEXT, and the Practical Social

Education Research Center of the National Educational Policy Research.

(2) Role and organization of local governments

The role of the prefectural government is to assist each municipality and to cover wide regional activities. In addition, the municipal board of education will directly support the community's social educational activities. An original task of municipalities not entrusted to prefectures, is to establish community learning centers. The role of municipalities is also the support for after school learning activities for children and support for the utilization of learning outcomes through social education.

In recent years, there are cases where the social education administration is transferred from the board of education to a general division according to the administrative and financial reforms and also the decentralization of authority. In addition, efforts similar to social education are being developed as "citizen collaborations" that cooperate with each other, sharing the purpose with companies, non-profit organizations, local residents, and promoting town development proactively. Although these are also related to human resource development to promote the regional creation and promotion of a network type administration, they could be good opportunities to reconsider the significance and role of social education administration without being bound by the characteristics of conventional social education.

(3) Social education finance and its planning

Expenditure on social education expenses should be considered in relation to its planning formulated by the central and local governments. The proportion of expenses for social education is less than 10% of total education expenditure. Also, the proportion of expenses to social education by central and local public bodies depends largely on their financial situation. The Social Education Law stipulates that the state will provide financial assistance to local governments, but this support system is struggling under the current serious situation of local finances. According to the growing needs for social education in a lifelong learning society, it is desirable to ensure stable financial resources in the future. However, creative ingenuity by effective and efficient methods is also necessary. There are local governments that try to solve these issues by utilizing private funds through public-private partnership, rather than covering everything with public expenses.

(4) Activities of social education related organizations

Social education related organizations are not under public control and are partnering with social education facilities. They include the Parent Teacher Association (PTA), the Children's Association, the Sports Boys' Association, Youth Organizations, the Boy and Girl Scouts, and Non-profit Organizations. These are operated autonomously without interference or control over the contents of activities and organizations by the central and local governments. The Law also prohibits the control by the governments through financial assistance to social education-related organizations under the principle of "no support, no control". However, after the law was amended in 1959, it was permitted to subsidize them after listening to the opinions of the board of social education committee.

5. Collaboration of School, Family, Community and Social Education

In recent years, social education policies are being developed focusing on enhancing the educational potential of society as a whole through cooperation between schools, families, and community and creating a mechanism for circulating learning outcomes in the region. It is urged to raise the awareness of the people involved in schools to clearly fulfill their roles and responsibilities toward the realization of educational purposes as stipulated by FLE. The Social Education Law also encourages projects to utilize learning outcomes of social education for schools and communities, prescribing the promotion of such collaboration. When the school collaborates and cooperates with the community and provides educational activities, the social education supervisor can advise according to the request of the school. Many of these initiatives are carried out through the participation of local people as volunteers, so the training of coordinators and enhancement of training programs become essential. In the future, the promotion of regional school collaborative activity will continue to spread.

Column-7: Lifelong Education

Education is widely provided in schools and as social education. People can learn in formal opportunities or informally. Such a system is called as lifelong learning and is defined as learning that takes place throughout the life, in school, at home, in the society, cultural, sports and recreation, volunteer activities, job training at companies, and hobbies (MEXT).

Lifelong education means the opportunities and system to be prepared by the government while lifelong learning is an expression from the viewpoint of learners. Usually, the role of the government is to realize a lifelong learning society, but it is not discussed so frequently. Thus, it has been noticed much more than ever the importance to arrange a social environment where people can learn autonomously through their life.

Such a policy has been recognized since 1973 when OECD pointed out the importance of "recurrent education". So many countries are asked to reform the employment system for the sake of the convenience of learning and on the other hand, educational institutions are asked to provide an effective curriculum for learners, particularly those in higher education.

As stated above, the range of lifelong education is extremely wide, the Japanese government has promoted several kinds of policies, for example, establishing the University of the Air, enhancing social education, supporting home education and so on. Nowadays, universities provide extension program certificates for working adults which are available to develop their career.

Another type of school education is also required to respond to the needs of local learners. Providing school facilities, correspondence schools, and evening classes are convenient for senior people.

School education is required to provide lifelong learning, but educational resources are not sufficient. Teachers, schools and local governments must increase the motivation of people to learn through their lifetime and support their learning as much as possible.

Part 2

Educational Administration

Chapter 7. Role of the State

The official actors of educational administration in Japan are central and local governments, and accordingly, the educational administration system of Japan is composed of central and local levels. This chapter provides an overview of the central system focusing on the function of the Ministry of Education, as the local system will be introduced in a following chapter.

1. The Role of Central Government

One of the most prominent characteristics of Japanese educational administration is seen in its unforced administrative method called "the administration based on guidance and advice." Article 48 of Law concerning the Organization and Operation of Local Educational Administration (LCOOLEA) defines that the higher-level organization of educational administration can provide necessary guidance, advice, or assistance to the lower-level organization, which limits the commitment of the central government's involvement with local educational administration to "necessary guidance, advice, or assistance." Before the World War II, educational administration was defined as a duty of the state, and local governments conducted educational affairs on behalf of the central government. After the War, however, educational administration was redefined as a local affair, so now local governments conduct educational affairs in various, autonomous ways.

Under such trends, the major roles of the central government on educational administration can be categorized into three areas: constructing the system framework, setting of central standards, and assisting the consolidation of educational conditions. For example, the "6-3-3-4-year school system" (6-year primary; 3-year lower secondary; 3-year upper secondary and 4-year university) is one of the most fundamental educational systems that the central government constructs. Regarding the central standards set by the central government, standards for establishment of schools, and course of study are major examples.

As an example of the assistance for the consolidation of educational conditions, the central government makes budget contributions for teacher salaries and school building construction. In order to fulfill these roles, the central government amends the laws, conducts projects with central budgets, and provides guidance and advice to local educational administrative bodies such as the board of education. Through these administrative works, the central-level educational administration tries to "comprehensively formulate and implement education measures in order to provide equal opportunities in education and to maintain and raise education standards throughout the country" (Article 16 (2), FLE, revised in 2006).

In a broader definition, the central educational administration is composed of Cabinet, Prime Minister, Minister of Education, and Ministry of Education, Culture, Sports, Science and Technology (MEXT). Centrally significant issues shall be discussed and implemented by advisory councils set under the Cabinet and Prime Minister, such as the Central Commission on Educational Reform (2000-01: proposed amendments to the FLE) and the Council for Revitalization of Education (2013-present: discussing the plan of educational reform in the 21st century). However, in a narrower definition, it is the MEXT that is in charge of central educational administration as seen below.

2. Ministry of Education, Culture, Sports, Science and Technology (MEXT)
(1) Restructuring from Ministry of Education to MEXT

Originally, the Ministry of Education was established in 1871 as a specialized organization of educational affairs. The establishment of the Ministry of Education has led to the creation of a centralized system of educational administration, under which all educational institutes across the nation and their educational contents are supervised by the central government. MEXT was launched in January 2001 through the Reform of Government Ministries, by integrating the former Ministry of Education with the existing Science and

Technology Agency. The purpose of this integration was to make it easier for MEXT to achieve its two major goals: to create an "education-aspired nation" and to develop it as a "science and technology-oriented nation."

This reform proceeded under the slogan of "from administrative initiative to political initiative" in order to reconsider the conventional, post-war system of educational administration that had been led by the central government. After the reform, the organization of the ministry was restructured and the positions of political appointment were increased as explained below (cf. Articles 16-17 in Central Government Organization Act).

(2) Structure of MEXT

After the Reform of Government Ministries in 2001, the organizational structure of MEXT was reconstructed as seen in Fig. 7-1. The number of bureaus, divisions and offices has been decreased by 30-40% in order to reduce inefficiency of the vertically segmented administrative system. Two Senior Vice-Ministers and two Parliamentary Secretaries are allocated under the Minister, and these five positions are political appointments. Together with an Administrative Vice-Minister and two Deputy Director Generals, these eight posts compose the leadership of MEXT.

The organization of MEXT has three major bodies: the Minister's Secretariat, Bureaus, and Commissioners. The Minister's Secretariat is in charge of general affairs, external affairs, and internal adjustments. Each Bureau has its own specialized area and works directly with the stakeholders of that specific area, such as local teachers at schools. There are two commissioners, one for Cultural Affairs and another for the Japan Sports Agency established outside the main body of MEXT. In addition to these organizations, there are Special Institutions and Organizations under MEXT's Jurisdiction. Special Institutions are considered "quasi-commissioners" and are highly specialized such as the Japanese Central Commission for UNESCO. Governmental think-tanks for policy planning and making, such as the National Institute for Educational

Policy Research, is located as one of Organizations under MEXT's Jurisdiction.

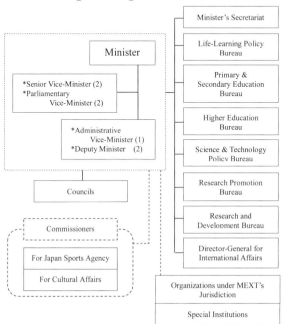

Fig. 7-1 Organization Chart of MEXT

(Source: Prepared by author from MEXT HP and Cabinet Secretariat HP)

(3) Responsibility and duty of MEXT

MEXT is in charge of educational administrative affairs which are defined by Article 3 of Act for Establishment of MEXT. According to the legal definition, three major duties of MEXT are (1) to encourage human development, by education and lifelong learning rich in humanity and creativity, (2) to promote academic research and culture, and (3) to implement comprehensive policies for developing science, technology and sports. As stated in this law, MEXT policies shall cover a broad range of public services, not only education but also academic research, culture, science and technology, and sports. This section provides a brief overview of the main functions and responsibility of the Minister of Education and MEXT.

a. Minister's function and responsibility

According to Article 10 of the Central Government Organization Act, the Minister of Education shall superintend MEXT's affairs, supervise its public services, and manage educational administration at the central level. Hence, the minister is given authority such as: (1) to submit a proposal and ask for a cabinet meeting in order to establish, revise or abolish an Act or Cabinet Order; (2) to issue a Ministerial Ordinance as an order from the Ministry; and, (3) to request a budget from the Minister of Finance.

b. MEXT's function and responsibility

Under the duties introduced above, MEXT is expected to conduct various kinds of affairs as defined in Article 4 of the Act for Establishment of MEXT. There are 97 items included in this Article. For example, there are several items related to planning policies, managing duties, and setting central standards (e.g. Standards for Establishment of Schools), several other items related to the non-authoritarian mechanism of guidance, advice, and assistance (e.g. guidance and advice on management of school environment), and other items based on governmental power such as permission (e.g. textbook certification).

c. Councils

A council is an advisory body for the minister as defined by Article 10 of the Central Government Organization Act. A council is in charge of the study and deliberation of significant matters for central educational policy and is expected to submit policy reports. The purpose of the council system is to introduce specialized knowledge and experience to the policy making process from experts' perspectives in various fields. Council members shall be selected among not only academic researchers, but in accordance with the purpose of the council above, experts from the private sector, NGOs, or any other profession may become members to discuss policy issues.

There are two major categories of councils. One is to propose policy recommendations through the study and deliberation of a specific policy issue. The other is to discuss the legitimacy of specific administrative dispositions. The CCE is an example of the former type of council. It was established during the Government Reform in 2001 by restructuring the existing seven councils: Central Council for Education (CCE), Lifelong Learning, Science and Industrial Education, Curriculum, Teacher Training, University, and Health and Physical Education. Today, the CCE is composed of four sectional committees: Committees for Educational System, Lifelong Learning, Primary and Secondary Education, and University. Each committee studies and deliberates the significant issues of each area to publish policy recommendations.

As for the latter type of council, councils such as Textbook Authorization Research Council and Council for University Chartering and School Juridical Person are in charge of legitimacy checks. These councils and their reports do not have legal binding power. However, from the perspective of keeping objectivity and fairness on a certain administrative disposition, the council's recommendation is generally recognized with respect.

3. Philosophy of Educational Administration in Japan

As mentioned above, one characteristic of educational administration in Japan is that local governments are responsible for education, while the central government is mainly conducting non-authoritative actions such as "guidance, advice, and assistance" to local governments. Such characteristics are derived from reflections on the educational administration system before the World War II.

There were four characteristics of educational administration before the War. Firstly, there was a centralized system centered on the Ministry of Education and the Ministry of the Interior, and the domination of education by central and local bureaucrats. The central government, not the local government, was in charge of education. Education was done through local bureaucracy such as local administrators (Hokkaido minister, prefectural governors) who were an institution of the central government.

Secondly, it adopted the commands of the Emperor, that is, in the form of the Royal Decree. This means that education did not depend on the law made by Congress in order to avoid education problems being influenced by political party politics.

Thirdly, there was no independent educational administrative agency. The local educational administration was subordinate to the general administration. Basically, the secretary of provincial affiliation was under the command and supervision of the Minister of the Interior, but for education, he was under the direction and supervision of the Minister of Education. The academic affairs division, like the internal affairs department and the police department, was a subsidiary body of the local minister.

Finally, there was a top-down command line between the central government and prefectures / municipalities, and command and supervision was done through a network of visiting school officials located in rural areas.

For such pre-war educational administration, the principle of educational administration was changed after the World War II. Centralized educational administration and bureaucratic domination were changed to decentralized educational administration. Education was decided not by the Emperor's orders but by the law prescribed by the Diet since it had become the highest institution of central rights and became the only legislative body. While the prewar educational administration was subordinate to the general administration, after the war it was independent from the general administration. The educational administration before the World War II directed and supervised education, but after the war, educational expertise and autonomy became respected.

Before the war in Japan, education was one of the measures utilized for

Chapter 7. Role of the State 137

political power in an absolute system to enrich the state and strengthen military power. Furthermore, the educational administration was a system for allowing all citizens to receive such education. On the contrary, the educational administration after the war was for the government to guarantee the right to receive education under the principle of the sovereignty of the people.

4. Relationship between Central and Local Governments

In this way, from the viewpoint of principle and mechanism, the educational administration in Japan is decentralized, democratic and non-authoritarian.

However, in fact, under the context of educational administration which is the Ministry of Education - prefecture board of education - municipal board of education - public school, there are various regulations under the name of "guidance, advice, and aid." This has been pointed out critically as a "country-local relationship" like "seniority" with "substantial enforcement". This implies that the involvement of the government and its finances have a great influence on the local educational administration.

(1) State involvement

In 1999, the "Act on the Improvement of Related Laws to Promote Decentralization" ("Decentralization Acts") was established. Prior to that, not only in the education field, the centralized system for each ministry and agency was strong. Here, "delegated institution affairs" was playing a major role. The institutional delegation affairs delegated and executed the work of the central government to the municipalities, and when executing the delegated affairs, the municipalities were supposed to receive comprehensive command and supervision of the central government.

In addition, a chief education officer, a municipal official of the prefecture, was approved by the Minister of Education, and the education chief of municipalities was required to be approved by the prefectural board of education. The system of requiring the approval of the higher-level institution to appoint key persons within the local education administration has been criticized as a special system not found in other administrative fields, and as a symbol of the centralized character of educational administration. Furthermore, according to the principle of educational administration as independent from general administration, the involvement of the head of the local body and the citizens was eliminated. With this, the relationship of the Ministry of Education - prefecture board of education - municipal board of education - public school was strengthened.

Under the "Decentralization Acts" in 1999, institutional reforms were implemented in which such involvement by the central government in local governments was reduced. First, "delegated institution affairs" was abolished, and it was arranged into statutory entrusted work that carries out the affairs of the central government based on the law and autonomous affairs that transfer as administrative affairs of the local government. In the field of educational administration as well, approval of IEIs etc. was regarded as statutory entrusted affairs. Also, several administrative affairs, such as the formation of school ages, designation of school attendance, and administrative affairs concerning standard approval of class organization, became autonomous affairs. The approval of the appointment of the chief education officer was also abolished. Furthermore, involvement of MEXT in local board of education committees and prefectural boards of education in the municipal board of education were reduced. For example, the text of the Educational Governing Body Act has been revised to "can do" necessary guidance, advice and assistance from the provision that the guidance, advice or assistance necessary "is taken".

However, in the revision of the Educational Governing Body Act in 2007, the authority of the State was strengthened. In the case of a violation of laws by a board of education or neglect, in order to urgently protect the life, body and educational rights of students, the MEXT can provide the local board of education with "instructions" or "request for correction" (Article 50 of the same law). The background of this revision is the heightened social criticism of boards of education. Because concern over the dysfunction of boards of education was rising, with cases in which the board of education took inappropriate measures against suicide by children caused by bullying, and due to the increase in the average age of municipal education board members.

(2) Impact of financial system

Another thing that has a major influence on the relationship between the central government and local governments is the mechanism of educational finance. The state provides cash to local governments to achieve specific policy objectives. This is called central treasury expenditure. There are roughly three kinds of central treasury expenditure issued from the State to the local governments in the education field, subsidies and allotments to be delivered with limited use and local allocation tax grants with unrestricted use. (Detailed commentary on educational finance is given in Chapter 9, Part 2)

Subsidies and allotments are budgets of MEXT and are used to realize equal opportunities for education, to promote educational policies aimed at by the central government, and filling in financial differences among regions. Subsidies and allotments under the jurisdiction of MEXT are said to demonstrate their influence on local governments, because many of them are paid for local governments. Among them, subsidies for salaries of teachers and staff, the cost of school buildings constructions and renovations of public primary and lower secondary schools are large in amount and the criteria is strictly determined. On the other hand, grants allocated from local taxes are under the jurisdiction of the Ministry of Internal Affairs and Communications (MIC), which oversees local administrative and financial affairs. However, there is no need to pay the grant in accordance with the calculation by MIC, and is treated as general revenue that the district can freely use.

Focusing on the mechanism of educational administration, the relationship between MEXT, local boards of education and heads of local bodies is important. But considering finances as well, complex relationships emerge, involving actors such as Ministry of Finance (MOF) and MIC. MOF has jurisdiction over the budget of the state including MEXT. Under the goal of central fiscal consolidation, the MOF is in a position opposing MEXT. MIC has a strong influence on educational administration in terms of the calculation of local tax allocation. For example, in 2006, a reform proposal to devalue the ratio of the treasury's share in expenditure for compulsory education from 1/2 to 1/3 was discussed. At that time, there was a conflict between Ministry of Public Management, Home Affairs, Posts and Telecommunications (MIC) on the side of local governments, which requested the abolition of the system and transfer of tax sources, and the MEXT wanting to maintain state burden. As a result, the share of the central treasury burden was devalued from 1/2 to 1/3 as planned.

As an overall flow, financial resources for compulsory education are being transformed into local allocation tax subsidies that are under the jurisdiction of the MIC, not subsidies and contributions that are included in the budget of MEXT. This is progress of decentralization in the sense that it improves local discretion. On the other hand, it can also be a cause of lower educational standards and regional disparities by using the budget calculated as educational expenditure on non-education related expenses.

As described above, it is difficult to explain all the intricacies of the relationship between the central government and local governments in Japanese educational administration with a simple binary confrontation and whether it is an equal or a controlled relationship. Fiscal aid for equality of educational opportunities is coincidental with the involvement of the central government and independence from the general administration creates internal relations of educational administration. In the context of the decentralization of administration in general, although the discretion of boards of education expanded, their distrust has been reinforced by the involvement of the state again.

Considering educational administrative philosophy and operation, the intermingling of involvement and support and social trends continue to change the structure and operation of educational administration.

Chapter 8. Local Educational Administration

1. The Principle of the Postwar Local Educational Administration Reform and its Transition

(1) Local educational administration reform just after the war

Local educational administration changed completely after the World War II. In the pre-war period, the task of education basically belonged to the central government and some tasks were delegated to the local government under the central government's strict control. The local government was not deemed as independent and tasks related to education were undertaken by the prefectural governor nominated by the Minister of Home Affairs. In the municipalities, the head of municipality carried out education tasks under the direct control and supervision of the Minister of Education and the prefectural governor. Primary and lower secondary school teachers were appointed by prefectural governors. Head of municipality had school administrative committee. The committee could express opinions when required. In other words, educational administration was very much centralized and implemented by not a single organization, but with other departments.

After the war, education was considered a local, original task and a new system was introduced based on the following three principles, firstly, self-government, secondly, people's autonomy, and thirdly, independence from other fields of educational administration. The board of education was established by "the Board of Education Law" in 1948 to ensure these principles. It was not only in the prefecture but at the municipality level according to the two-layer system of local government. In this section, these three principles are explained.

Generally, local autonomy includes the following two aspects, autonomy for the local government and for its people. Self-government is for organizational performance and the people's autonomy means people can act and choose what they need and local politics and administration should always reflect their opinions.

In the context of educational administration, self-government means the local board of education is not controlled by the central government and operates independently. The relationship between the Ministry of Education and prefecture and municipality education boards should be understood as horizontal. As a result, local board of education could be given the useful information and advice when needed and at no time could a higher ranking organization intervene in their operation.

A typical system of people's autonomy was local elections. The education committee was to be elected as the representatives of the people. Committee size differed, 7 in prefecture and 5 in municipalities by the Board of Education Law, and in each committee one was from the local assembly and the rest were elected by local citizens. Additionally, the "direct claim system" should be noticed. According to the current Law concerning Organization and Operation of Local Education Administration (LCOOLEA), when 1/3 of the electorate claim, and 3/4 of assembly members agreed, the education committee and the chief education officer could be dismissed.

Table 8-1 shows the distribution of power among the local government and that for education which could be recognized as being relatively independent. (For details, see section 2)

Table 8-1 Relation between General and Educational Administration

	General local politics	Local educational politics
Legislation	Local Assembly member of the local assembly	Board of Education Education Committee
Administration	Local government head Local government offices	Chief Education Officer Board of Education Office
Justice	--	--

Furthermore, the function of the board of education was supported by two principles, layman control and professional leadership.

An board of education was constituted by citizen's representatives and education committee was not required to have any qualifications nor experience (layman), but as a citizen, they were expected to voice their opinions and plans on behalf of the people as a whole. Layman control meant that education should be controlled by the local people and this is an actual pattern of democracy in education.

On the other hand, professional leadership meant that the chief education officer who had experience and knowledge about educational administration maintains leadership for policy-making and its implementation. This distribution of roles (checks and balances) was expected to be effective and as a result was satisfactory.

However, it is a fact that the board of education did not run as was expected. Members of the committee were not full time staff, but the chief education officer was. As a result, the chief education officer was likely to lead the plan and after the decision he/she actually managed and controlled the all tasks of the board of education. This situation without a basic philosophy to balance the will of the people and experts with rich experience of education became obvious and this point emerged as a serious problem to be solved.

(2) Legislation of LCOOLEA and its revision

Looking back on the local educational administrative system after World War II, three major reforms have been undertaken. The first one was the enactment of the "Board of Education Law" in 1948, shortly after the war. Under this Law, The board of education was introduced to realize democracy in education with three principles, and the election of education committee members took place by the local people.

The second stage began after the enactment of the LCOOLEA in 1956, and consequently, the former Board of Education Law was repealed, although

Chapter 8. Local Educational Administration 145

public opinion was strongly against this reform. This newly introduced law changed the election system for the education committee members to a procedure in which the head of the local government appoint them. In addition, the LCOOLEA introduced the approval system for appointing the chief education officer. Such appointment in the municipal needed the prefectural chief education officer's approval and the Minister of Education did it in the case of the prefecture. Furthermore, the Minister of Education was given the power of "corrective requirement" to ask the local board of education to amend the implementation of administration and also the prefectural board of education could do it to the municipal board of education as well.

Other revised points were, firstly, to abolish the power of the board of education over budgets and finances, secondly, to transfer compulsory school personnel power to the prefecture from the municipality. In this way, the LCOOLEA, after the former Board of Education Law was repealed, actually changed the basic policy of education administration just after the war.

Since then, this Law has been amended little by little up to the recent year, and the enactment of the Decentralization Acts, 1999, educational administration was affected to be revised accordingly.

The Decentralization Acts asked to revise 475 laws as an omnibus, including the Local Government Act to promote local autonomy, especially self-government. Although its contents are diverse, the most noteworthy was that the abolition of "assigned function" which asked the central government for control and supervision. This reform made local governments undertake just a "statutory entrusted function" and its original tasks. As a result of this reform, the local government function involved by the central government has remarkably reduced.

According to the enactment of the Decentralization Acts, the actual range of local government has increased, and the role of the central government dropped down from 80% to nearly 40% in the prefecture.

As for education office work, the designation of school attendance etc. was reclassified as a "self-governing function" apart from the power engagement of central government.

Furthermore, the appointment approval system for chief education officer as well as corrective requirements by Minister of Education was repealed when this Act launched (However, the ordering power from upper ranked organization was revived in 2007).

In spite of these reforms, the basic structure of the board of education has not changed so much since the enactment of the former LCOOLEA, but it was changed remarkably by the revision of it in 2014. This change could be called the third major reform of local educational administration.

2. Major Changes of LCOOLEA in 2014
(1) The Structure of the board of education before the major change of LCOOLEA

The structure and function of the board of education prior to this reform is shown in **Fig. 8-1**.

Firstly, "Board of Education" means the legislative body for educational policy, and this body normally consisted of 5 or 6 persons appointed by the governor or city mayor. A member among them was nominated and elected as the chair of board of education and was expected to perform as a mediator as well as the representative of that meeting. This meeting plays the same role as the local assembly apart from its size.

Secondly, local government officials carried out actual policies under the head of prefectures in general local politics. In the case of educational politics, such policy was decided by the board of education and was carried out by the office of the board of education and its chief education officer who was appointed by the board.

Fig. 8-1 Structure of the Board of Education (before 2014)

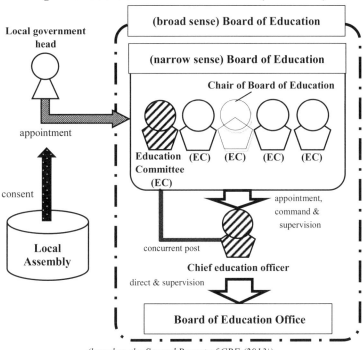

(based on the Second Report of CRE (2013))

In this way, decisions and their implementation were usually independent from other departments, for the sake of its sound development.

In addition, the "Board of education Office" was comprised of local government officials. Most of them were likely to engage in general office work, but some were employed to undertake the limited duties for inspection and advisory staff for school and social education. This "Board of Education Office" and "the (narrow sense) Board of Education" were called "the Board of Education" as a whole.

(2) Background of the major revision of LCOOLEA in 2014

The most possible reason why the board of education system should be revised is that the board of education had not performed its original role effectively. As already pointed out, the final decision of the (narrow sense) board of education was prepared by officials in advance and such meetings became just a formality. That means the public opinions among the local people were not reflected and this situation could be called the breaking down of people's autonomy.

In this circumstance, some academic staff of administrative study and others often insisted that the board of education was not necessary. They also insisted that the MEXT and the board of education had strong ties which obstructed the development of self government. In this context, they asked to abolish the board of education to realize the local autonomy.

Although these controversies had been taking place for a long time, the major change of the local educational system was brought about from another factor which no one could imagine, the case of the suicide of male student due to bullying at his school in Otsu City, Shiga Prefecture in October 2011. It received a lot of media attention and the board of education was criticized for not having taken any prompt action. Its leadership was blamed as well. Prime Minister, Shinzo Abe's Cabinet was keen to make use of this serious situation as a catalyst to reform the system to their liking.

In fact, the Council for Revitalization of Education (CRE) proposed the first report under the title of "Responding to Bullying" in February 2013 and "The Reform of the Board of education System" as a second report in April of the same year. These reports actually encouraged the reform of the board of education and MEXT also asked the Central Council for Education (CCE) to discuss the "the way of future local educational administration" in the same month. Surprisingly, the corresponding report was issued a short time later in December of the same year. From this quick response by the government, it could be assumed that there might be a strong interest in education and an intension to intervene in local educational administration by the Abe administration, which actually amended the FLE 2006. This commitment clearly led to a total revision of the system according to their policy.

(3) Contents of the revision of LCOOLEA, 2014

Fig. 8-2 Structure of the Board of Education (after 2014)

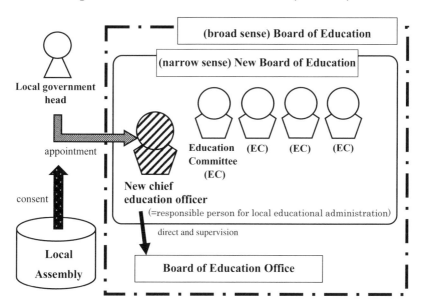

(based on the Second Report of CRE (2013))

1) Clarification of the persons responsible for local education Administration

The chairperson of board of education also holds the post of chief education officer appointed by the top of the local government. The posts used to be separate, one for the representative and the other for the top of the administrative department as described. However, the new system of one person occupying both posts is very effective to undertake their duty quickly and solve problems. At the same time, it is quite easy to know who is responsible for the local educational administration.

2) The head of local government more powerful

The head of the local government is elected by the people, and is responsible for the local administrations. Although education is expected to be implemented separate from others, the head of the local government, usually politicians, is given the power to affect local education by this revised Law.

a. Appointment of the chief education officer

The head of local government is able to appoint a chief education officer directly according to the revisions. Also the status of chief education officer becomes a special service position, and the Local Public Service Act is not applied. Although the chief education officer is a member of the board of education, its post is not deemed as an original member of the committee. This composition clarified the two principles of layman control and professional leadership, but the power of the chief education officer has also been strengthened more than ever. As a result, when selecting the new chief education officer, careful procedures such as making a presentation by the candidate are required. Although the term of office, four years, was initially the same as the former system, it became three years, a year shorter than the education committee, and was requested to strengthen their supervision of the education committee and the local assembly. While the authority of the chief education officer was strengthened, there were few changes to the duties of the education committee and the balance of power was greatly inclined to the professional leaders. In fact, the board of education has been deemed as an honorary board. Public local opinions have not been taken into account in discussions or in the process of policy-making, and the criticism is that it has lost substance and does not reflect the will of people. It is quite doubtful how far the checking function of the board of education can be performed.

b. Drawing up the general guideline

The need for drawing up general principles was newly added to Article 1 of the Partial Revision the LCOOLEA and this "general guideline" is to be decided by the head of local governments consulting with the synthetic education conference. However, it was also stated in Article 21 that the drawing of it is not the duty of the head of the local government on behalf of the board of education. In other words, it is emphasized that the authority of the head of local governments is similarly restricted as before. In addition, the general guideline only shows the target of education and provides the fundamental policy to be implemented and it does not regulate any aspects precisely.

c. Providing the synthetic education conference

The synthetic education conference is a meeting which the head of the local government organizes. Its purpose is "to promote educational administration that reflects the opinions of the people, by communicating sufficiently sharing the issues of the local education and its ideals." It was to be provided for all local governments with the presence of the head of local governments and the members of their education committees as a place for consultation and coordination among concerned agencies. The meeting can also invite stakeholders and academic experts and listen to their opinions if necessary.

Contents to be discussed at that conference are; (1) consultation on the formulation of general guidelines, (2) improvement of various conditions for education according to actual conditions in local areas, and discussion of the policy for promoting academic and cultural standards, and (3) consultation and necessary measures to be taken in emergency cases injury or death of children or its anticipation.

However, it is of concern that a much more powerful role of the head of local governments may infringe on the principle of the independence of educational administration from others and has also been criticized for political intervention in education. The board of education needs to once again be conscious of its role to ensure political neutrality. As mentioned above, the role of the education committee consisting of layman has been left unchanged which means it plays a diminished role due to the changing power of the chief education officer and the head of local government. It has long been pointed out that the people's autonomy in the activity of the board of education has become a lost substance and another revision is required to recover it role and to promote it further.

On the other hand, there is no doubt that the budgeting process for educational administration has become quicker because of the intervention of the head of local government. In particular, positive discussion has been rare in the board of education because of the huge budget, such as the expenditure for buildings and other facilities. In that sense, having close coordination with the head of the local government with budget authority could make this aspect more efficient.

3)Involvement in the local public body by the central government

It was clarified that the Minister of MEXT can give instructions to the board of education when it is urgently necessary to prevent the endangerment of a child's well-being, such as cases of bullying.

3. The Present Day Aspects of Local Education Administration
(1) The authority between the board of education and head of local governments

Although the new LCOOLEA stipulates the authorities of the board of education and the head of local government, the principle of independence of educational administration from general administration is still indicated, and many of the duties belong to the board of education. The authority of the head of local governments is limited as shown below (Article 22);

1. About the university

2. About the kindergarten and nursery center

3. About non-governmental school

4. Acquisition and disposal of educational property
5. Enter into contracts concerning matters pertaining to the affairs of the board of education
6. In addition to what is listed in the preceding items, enforcing the budget on matters pertaining to the affairs of the board of education

From these provisions, the power of the head of local governments is to be recognized as limited to university, certified centers for early childhood education and care, non-governmental schools, and municipality finances. On the contrary, the authority of the board of education covers a wider range as follows; establishment, management and abolition of schools, teacher personnel affairs, entrance / exit / transfer of infants, children and students, school curriculum and educational guidance, textbooks and other teaching materials, facilities and equipment maintenance, teacher training, school meal, social education, etc.

In this way, the board of education has an overwhelmingly wide range of authority compared to the head of local governments. However, the authority of the head of local governments is essentially important, and the board of education cannot unilaterally decide and implement educational policy, because the head of local government has financial authority. The head of local governments has the authority on budget, but the board of education does not. Thus, for example, even if the board of education decides to increase the number of computers at each school to promote Information and Communication Technology (ICT) education, it cannot be implemented without the approval of the head of the local government. In addition, he/she has authority to appoint members of education committees and consequently to affect the activities of the board of education.

This relation between them had not changed up to present day even after the revision of the LCOOLEA in 2014. In other words, even after the revision, the authority of the board of education is still wide, but the power of the head of local governments has been kept as is and has become much more powerful than ever.

(2) The current situation of the board of education

The number of boards of education is 47 for prefectures and 1,814 for municipalities (in May 2015).

Regarding their constitution, it was stipulated that their member composition could be diversified by the partial amendment of LCOOLEA in 2001. According to it, age, gender, occupation, etc. of the committee should be considered. Also, efforts were made towards appointing parents in 2007. In 2015, the number of female members was 2,749 (37.9%) and parents, 2,230 (30.7%), which was increasing year by year. As to the occupations, the majority are unemployed, 2,521 (34.7%). Also, 2,037 (28.1%) of the members had teaching experience, which may indicate that a certain number become members after retiring from teaching jobs (**Table 8-2**).

Table 8-2 Education Committee Occupation

Classification	Number	%
Doctor / Technician	1,750	24.1
Company executive	1,413	19.5
Agriculture and forestry	625	8.8
Store management	527	7.3
Others	421	5.8
Unemployed	2,521	34.7
(of the total number: Teachers' experience)	(2,037)	(28.1)
total	7,257	100

(prepared by the author based on MEXT "Educational Administration Survey in 2015")

Regarding the chief education officer, the number of females was 62 (3.6%), while parents were 50 (2.9%). Of the total (1,716) their average age was 59.3

Chapter 8. Local Educational Administration   155

years old. The chief education officer's former careers were 70.4% for experienced teachers, 80.2% for educational administrators, and 30.8% for general administrative experience. The career path to the chief education officer could be generally thought of as after starting as a teacher, passing through as a middle manager, temporarily transferred to an educational administrative position, then returned to a school as a managerial post, and after retiring he/she is likely to be appointed as a chief education officer. In some cases appointment from the general local government office or from the MEXT can be noticed.

(3) Duties and activities of the board of education

In this section the difference between prefectural and municipal boards of education is described, firstly. Although basic differences are hard to see, the notable legal difference between them is the appointment of teachers. Teachers of a municipal school are appointed by the prefectural board of education whose salary is paid by the prefecture, and the municipal board is asked to supervise their working process only.

Secondly, the main duty of prefectural and municipal education committee members is to attend board of education meetings convened by the chief education officer once or twice a month. There are "regular meetings" and "extraordinary meetings", and are binding with the attendance of more than half of the total members. Although the conference is open to the public in principle, it is not necessary to disclose it when dealing with personnel affairs or incidents. The chief education officer is asked to complete and publish the minutes promptly after the conference. Currently, many local governments have a homepage, and conference information and meeting minutes are openly available. The general agenda is as follows; personnel affair (school teachers hiring/transfer/promotion/demotion/change in employment status), construction and consolidation of schools, approval of laws and ordinances (New establishment and revision of regulations), budget proposal approval, formulation of educational policy, protection of cultural properties, and so on. In addition, urgent problems are discussed from time to time, for example, policy on library collections, method of announcing the survey results of the National Assessment of Academic Ability, measures concerning promotion of sports, and the adoption of compulsory education textbooks.

For discussion about education, the current situation of schools and its surroundings are quite essential for the members and they are asked to visit the schools, meet the principal, observe classrooms, and participate in regularly held ceremonies and school events. In addition to these activities, participation in various workshops and regional events are also recommended.

However, it is also true that there is a different atmosphere among the board of education conference. It can be supposed that the performance of the board of education is deemed as an honorary job, and in fact, sometimes opinions are not reflected at school. As to meeting agendas, members are only to pursue those prepared by board of education office, and not so many debates take place in general.

The background of these disparities arises from the fact that members themselves do not clearly understand their role. At the same time, the chief education officer and their office control the meeting and they do not expect an essential discussion among them. This is yet another reason for the committee being called a meaningless existence.

The board of education office is basically responsible for practical work according to the decision of the board of education. This aspect which supports its substantial performance depends on their full time activity. On the other hand, the members of committee are asked to do their job as a part time not as a full time staff. The tasks of the board of education follow a wide range of areas, from school education, social education, to sports, and culture. Also they have to always be aware of the latest information and are asked to respond to any situation in a short time. In these circumstances they have to perform properly according to the legislation and local rules and in an urgent case, the chief education officer is allowed to give instructions to the staff without having a formal meeting. When this kind of arbitrary decision is made, the chief education officer must report it at the board of education meeting afterwards and needs its approval.

The board of education office that carries out these substantive tasks and the chief education officer who directly manages a lot of judgments. This structure makes it possible to control the board of education.

(4) Future prospects

Looking back on current situation from the three principles of post-war regional educational administrative reform, it cannot be denied that the educational committee has been losing its essential meaning and also has failed to guarantee the importance of people's autonomy. After the World War II, education was regarded as a regional affair and the board of education system was introduced. The Decentralization Acts of 1999 encouraged the movement of local autonomy further. However, it was merely to promote self-governing, and people's autonomy was left behind after the repeal of the Board of Education Law of 1956. Certainly, the amendment of the LCOOLEA in 2014 was a conscious attempt at recovering the people's autonomy and to make the power of the head of local government stronger to secure the people's opinion for education. But that was a kind of rhetoric and it brought retrogress far from realizing the people's autonomy. It also brought about a risky situation where educational administration could be intervened by political forces, in particular by the ideas of the head of the local government. In that case, the continuity and stability of education may be impaired.

Another very serious disparity particular to rural areas needs to be pointed out. Since the progress of self-government means the recession of uniformed control from the central to local education administration, the diversity and the quality of local educational administration brought about a difference in local motivation and creativity. Furthermore, it is expected that it will become increasingly more pronounced due to the difference in response to the new system after 2014.

Chapter 9. Educational Finance

1. The Situation of Educational Expenditure

Compared with other OECD countries, Japan spends remarkably less on public education. According to a survey of OECD, in 2013, public expenditure on education as percentage of GDP was 3.5% in Japan, much less than the OECD average of 4.8% and was ranked 31st among 33 OECD nations (**Fig. 9-1**).

Fig. 9-1 Public Expenditure on Education as a Percentage of GDP, 2013

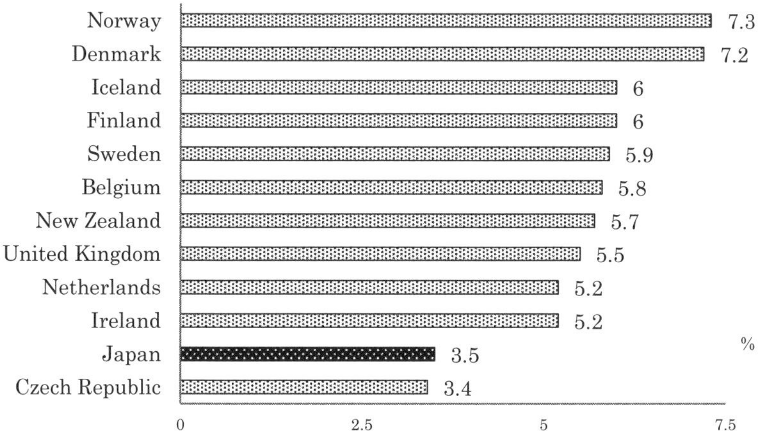

Norway	7.3
Denmark	7.2
Iceland	6
Finland	6
Sweden	5.9
Belgium	5.8
New Zealand	5.7
United Kingdom	5.5
Netherlands	5.2
Ireland	5.2
Japan	3.5
Czech Republic	3.4

(OECD *Education at a Glance 2016: OECD Indicators*, 2016)

Also, public expenditure on education as percentage of total public expenditure in Japan was ranked 28th at 8.1%, much less than the 11.2% average (**Fig. 9-2**).

Fig. 9-2 Public Expenditure on Education in Total Expenditure, 2013

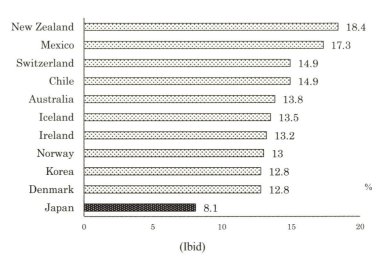

(Ibid)

The relationship of public expenditure and private spending on education in Japan in 2013 was 72% (OECD average 84%) and 28% (OECD average 16%) respectively. In primary and secondary education, public expenditure was 93% (OECD average 91%) and private was 7% (OECD average 9%). In higher education, public expenditure was 35% (OECD average 70%) and private was 65% (OECD average 30%). As compared with OECD countries, the ratio of public expenditure is less and the ratio of private spending is large. In particular, in higher education, the ratio of public expenditure is remarkably small and its dependence on private spending is very clear.

Regarding private spending on education, according to a Household budget survey of the Ministry of Internal Affairs and Communications statistical department, in 2014, the ratio that school expenses occupies in a labor (two or more persons') household's budget had become about 5.7%. According to "a child's learning expense survey" conducted by MEXT in 2014, it was 321,708 yen (US$ 2,925) for a child in public primary schools and 1,535,789 yen (US$ 13,962) for private schools.

Similarly, it costs 481,841 yen (US$ 4,380) for children in public lower secondary school as compared to 1,338,623 (US$ 12,169) yen for private lower secondary schools. Additionally, 409,979 yen (US$ 3,727) is payed for children in public upper secondary (day school), and 995,295 yen (US$ 9,048) for private upper secondary schools (day school). The survey calculated expenses as schooling expenses, school lunches, and expenses for out of school activities.

2. System of Educational Finance
(1)The central and local relationship to public finance

Of the total tax revenue generated in 2014, 61.6% came from national taxes and 38.4% came from provincial taxes. On the contrary, expenditure was 58.3% by state and 41.7% by local governments. In the case of expenditure on education, 12% is paid by the state and the rest by local governments. The financial structure is centralized where tax revenue mainly concentrates on a national level and afterwards is allotted to local governments.

As for local revenue in fiscal 2014, the percentage of provincial tax was only 36.0% and the ratio of general finances was also only 56.1%. On the other hand, the ratio of the national subsidy was 11.3% and the ratio of prefectural bonds was 15.2%. It is so clear that the local financial resources are depending on a national treasury subsidy and local bonds.

(2) The budget of the MEXT

The estimated budget for MEXT in fiscal 2017 is about 5,309,700 million yen. It is fifth largest scale among the central offices, after the Ministry of Health, Labor and Welfare, a Department of Treasury, the Ministry of Internal Affairs and Communications, and the Ministry of Land, Infrastructure, Transport and Tourism and its share is about 5.4% of the total national expenditure.

The main beneficiaries are compulsory education (28.7%), grants for state university corporation (20.6%), expenses for developments in technology (16.2%), grants for private school (8.1%), and support for upper secondary students (7.2%).

(3) Local school expense

In 2014, educational expenses occupied 16.9% of local governments' total purpose-oriented expenditures, while social welfare expenses topped the list at 24.8% (**Table 9-1**).

Table 9-1 Status of the Amount of a Purpose-oriented Expenditure (2014)

Section	%	Section	%
General secretary	10.0	Engineering works	12.2
Social welfare	24.8	Fire brigade	2.2
Sanitation	6.2	Police	3.2
Labor	0.4	Education	16.9
Agriculture, forestry & fishery	3.4	Public debts	13.6
Commerce and industry	5.6	Others	1.5

(Ministry of Internal Affairs and Communications "White Paper on Local Public Finance" 2016)

In the case of expenditure for school education in local finances in general, expenses for primary and lower secondary schools accounted for about 50%. This is because all prefectures have to pay the salaries of the staff at compulsory schools provided by the municipalities. This is nearly 40 % of their entire budget.

Regarding municipality finances, social education and health and physical education are at the top of the list. Although these programs make up only about 1% of a prefecture's budget respectively, municipalities pay 18.1% for social education and 21.4% for health and physical education because they are basically responsible for undertaking these programs (**table 9-2**).

Chapter 9. Educational Finance   163

Table 9-2 Breakdown of Educational Expenses by Type (2014, %)

	Prefectures	Municipalities	Net Total
Educational in general	19.2	13.5	17.1
Primary school	31.1	24.6	29.0
Lower secondary school	18.5	14.2	17.1
Upper secondary school	19.2	2.7	13.5
Schools for special needs	7.6	0.4	5.2
Kindergarten	0.0	4.2	1.5
Social education	1.6	18.1	7.3
Health and physical education	1.2	21.4	8.2
University and college	1.5	0.7	1.2

(White Paper on Local Public Finance, 2016)

The expense for personnel as a whole was 22.9%, but in particular, educational personnel constituted the largest portion at 61%. In prefectures, the ratio of the personnel expense in the whole expenditure was 27.2% and 80.7% for educational personnel expenses. Expense for educational personnel is the largest in prefecture as well. Similarly, the personnel expense was 15.8% of the total expenditures of municipalities, and 23.1% was for education. Since education is undertaken by human resources, and therefore providing a considerable number of teachers and staff is inevitable, it is necessary to review the financial structure and how local and state organizations should share that responsibility in the future (**Table 9-3**).

Table 9-3 Breakdown of Educational Expenses by Purpose (2014, %)

	Prefectures	Municipalities	Net Total
Personnel	80.7	23.1	61.0
Goods purchasing	3.2	32.7	13.5
Maintenance	0.2	1.6	0.7
Subsidizing, supporting etc.	11.4	8.7	10.1
Ordinary construction work	3.9	32.2	13.7
Others	0.6	1.7	1.0

(Ibid)

(4) National treasury subsidy

Simply put, the national treasury is and encompassing term. It consists of national obligatory shares, commissioning expenses, incentives for specific policies, and financial assistance distributed from the national government to local governments for spending on specific purposes. An outline of the national treasury subsidy concerning school education is as follows.

a. National obligatory share

The national obligatory share is a treasury charge for the official works which local governments are legally bound carry out and are related to the interests of both the central and local government in order to be managed smoothly (Local Public Finance Law). They are a central government's share of compulsory education expenses (the salary for school staff of state compulsory schools), maintenance of school facilities, for the occasional grant for schools affected by natural disasters, and to support the promotion of education for students with special needs. The national government is responsible for about a half or one third of the total expenses.

b. Subsidies from the national treasury

Subsidies from the national treasury are incentives for specific policies or financial assistance for local government (Local Public Finance Law). There are subsidies for expenses related to promoting cooperation between school, home, and community, to develop the educational support system and school facilities, etc.

(5) Distribution of the local allocation tax

The Local allocation tax is an intrinsic revenue source of local governments in order to adjust imbalances in tax revenue among local governments and to guarantee revenue sources so that every local government across the country can provide a consistent level of public services. Its fiscal source is based on a fixed percentage of national taxes, 32% for income and liquor tax, 34% for corporate tax, 22.3% for consumption tax, 25% for tobacco tax, and the total amount of local corporate tax in 2014.

This grant to local governments is the amount after the standard government earnings amount is deducted from the amount of standard financial demand. A distribution of this tax is not distributed to the local governments where the standard government earnings amount exceeds the amount of standard financial demand. The standard government earnings amount is calculated by adding the local transfer tax etc. to 75% of the standard local government estimated tax revenues. The amount of standard financial demand is calculated by multiplying the measurement unit by the unit cost of every administration item multiplied by a correction factor. The measurement unit (number of school staff, students, classes, and number of schools) and the unit cost are authorized by law (Local Allocation Tax Law).

(6) Issues of decentralization

The fiscal administration of Japan is a centralized system in which tax revenue concentrates on national government. Fiscal resources are delivered from central to local governments by the national treasury subsidy and the distribution of the local allocation tax. However, as regional differences have clearly been found and the gaps have become wider, it is necessary to give them the power of autonomy and of implementing their original fiscal management in a changing society. From fiscal 2003 to 2005, the transfer of revenue sources from central to local government, the retrenchment of a national treasury disbursement, and the retrenchment of the distribution of the local allocation tax were performed integrally at the same time and reform of the fiscal administration to strengthen local financial ability by them was also tried. However, as previously pointed out, local fiscal resources are vulnerable as a whole and depend on national fiscal resources. Therefore, a decentralized system is still required in spite of this reform.

If local governments depend on the central government's financial resources, there is no other way but to just requisition the central government all the time. In other words, the trend for the national government to control local governments will become stronger without any reform to affirm the autonomy of local governments. In this way, it is required to establish a fiscal system that allows local governments to operate autonomously while trying to secure financial resources nationwide in order not to produce a gap between the fiscal resources of local governments.

3. Educational Finance Issues
(1) Effective measures against child poverty

In the first decade of the 21st century, there has been a clearly recognizable disparity in society and an effective policy to correct it has been tried. This is also a serious problem in education as well. A system has been developed to subsidize impoverished families to improve school attendance and the performing rate of such families has been increasing. In fact, school attendance aid used to be 6.1% in 1995 but ascended to 15.4% in nearly twenty years (MEXT, "Survey on the status of enrollment aid implementation" 2013). This shows the number of impoverish families has steadily increased.

The correlation between a family's level of income and the child's academic achievements is also clear. These families cannot afford the financial burdens of sending their child to upper schools (high schools and universities) and as a result, the child is given limited job opportunities with a certain standard of working conditions. Thus, the negative cycle of poverty that is difficult to slip out in and of itself has become much more serious. Obviously poverty affects the future of children. In this context, it is required as an urgent topic that the central government takes action and fund child anti-poverty programs. The central government has initiated various relief measures for low-income households to ease the financial burdens of high secondary schools etc. by founding a upper secondary attendance support system. It is required to enrich, not only economic assistance programs, but assistance in connection with education, and to finance expenditures towards the dissolution of Japan's problem of child poverty from now on.

The principle of tuition free compulsory education should be thorough and the potential of expanding free school before and after compulsory education should be examined in efforts to enrich child anti-poverty programs.

(2) Evidenced-based educational policy

In order to promote the financial policy including the child anti-poverty program mentioned above, it is necessary to form and implement the politics which achieves the target and to develop its effectiveness. So, a policy deployment is required to be based on evidence. At Fiscal System Council, the following has been repeatedly discussed, "About an education policy, in order to consider it as a very efficient and effective investment, it is necessary to repeat the controversy based on clear evidence, and to establish a PDCA (Plan-Do-Check-Action) cycle."

It is an important policy for the state to fix class sizes in school and the number of school staff for they are closely related to expenditure, and in fact, this dispute has been ongoing between the MEXT and the Department of

Treasury. MEXT is asking for an increase in school staff in order to improve the educational conditions of a school, but the Department of Treasury always ask whether an increase in the number of school staff leads to improved academic outcomes or not. This is an ongoing, severe dispute between the two agencies.

Since it is difficult to clearly show education results, in particular as numeric figures, there is the critique that education policy is implemented with an ambiguous accession target. In a severe financial situation, decisions regarding education policy based on evidence will be required much more in future. For that purpose, it is necessary to develop research which clarifies evidence. Also, in order to obtain the understanding of taxpayers, it is important to build a system focused on accountability and school educational outcomes.

Column-8: School Facilities
1. The Facility

The standard regulations of school regulates that schools should have class rooms (ordinary and special ones), a library, a nurse's room, and a room for teachers. In addition a playground and a gymnasium are required except for special circumstances. The size of school buildings and playgrounds is also regulated.

There should also be a science room, a music room, a fine arts room, and a computer room as a special room. Libraries should have various kinds of books such as story books, picture books, illustrated books, encyclopedias, and dictionaries which satisfy the students' desire for learning. A nursing teacher is provided to undertake a medical check, consultation and emergency care. There is an education consulting room where a school counselor is on stand-by for student health consultations. Teaching materials and aids are supplied for teaching preparation in the teachers' room. As the teachers stay together in their room, they exchange various information each other. Many schools also have a principal's room.

2. The Issues of Facility Arrangement

Air conditioning units for cooling and warming rooms and anti-earthquake facilities have not yet been established in many schools. It is an important issue as is establishing facilities that support students' independent learning activities. The first is facilities to enable students a multi learning style approach such as team teaching, individual learning, and group learning. The second is to expand and improve the information environment such as an information network, computers and projectors. The third is to enrich the science room. The fourth is to develop education for international understandings. The fifth is to expand special education facilities and an environment in response to individual educational needs of students who require special support.

Chapter 10. Features of Educational Administration in Japan

1. Transition of the Role of the Central Government in Educational Administration

(1) Sprouting of modern educational administration system in Japan

This chapter begins by looking back at the historical circumstances of educational administration in Japan, and describes how those features have developed.

In the history of educational administration in Japan, many of its important aspects have been formed by the central government, not local governments. In other words, by promoting a powerful top-down educational administration, top priority was given to promote education among people for their literacy, to realize the unity of the people, and to cultivate human resources which would contribute to the effective operation of the state and the development of the Japanese society.

Educational administration did not start as an independent system to develop individual abilities as much as possible, but rather as a system within the management of the nation as a whole in order to prioritize the creation of manpower that fulfilled the interests of society and the state. In this way, the axis of centralization or decentralization becomes an important point in grasping the features of educational administration. At the same time, it also becomes another axis whether educational administration is independent from general administration or is subordinated and included within it.

After the Tokugawa era, Japan began to embark on the road to a modern state during the Meiji Restoration (1868). Like many other countries, education has been regarded as an important means of modernization. Therefore, priority was put on establishing a centralized system of educational administration. In 1871 the Ministry of Education was established. In the following year the Meiji government promulgated the first Education Code which was the regulation describing the composition of the Japanese school system. In the first Education

Code, a centralized educational system was designed, based on the French model at that time. It divided the nation geographically into 8 large school districts or university districts. Each large school district was subdivided into 32 middle school districts or secondary school districts. Each of those was further divided into 210 small school districts or primary school districts. The Ministry of Education was tasked with the oversight of all districts.

Additionally, organizations and positions that nationally control education were established nationwide. These include school supervisors, local officials, and school district secretaries. The goal of these organizations was to build a centralized management system specifically for education, independent of general administration. However, in reality, some local governments strongly opposed the financial burden of funding and maintaining schools without having control over educational content, so the idea of the first Education Code was never sufficiently developed.

(2) The establishment of a centralized system before the world war II

In 1879 a new regulation called the Liberal Education Order was drafted. Its aim was to control local educational administrations through a school committee system like the USA's boards of education system which was introduced to Japan after the World War II. Accordingly, the former system was abolished and it was decided, based on the revision of the general local system at that time, that municipalities e.g. cities, towns and villages be established as the basic organization and residents should elect the school committee members. This system could be regarded as the decentralization of educational administration.

However, this regulation was strongly criticized as having caused a decrease in the number of schools and a decline in the enrollment rate. It was abolished about one year later. In 1880, the Revised Educational Order was issued stating the powers of prefectural governors to appoint school committee members and municipal primary school teachers, and decide guidelines for local primary schools.

The centralized educational administrative system started from the end of the 19th century. Following the establishment of a cabinet system in the central government, Arinori Mori (1847 - 1889) was appointed as the first Minister of Education. In addition, under the Constitution of the Empire of Japan in 1889 and the Imperial Rescript on Education in 1890, a powerful centralized educational administration system was constructed which was expected to be controlled not by the law approved by the Parliament, but by the "orderism (rescriptism)" based on the orders of the Emperor.

Subsequently, the local system of educational administration was formed as a mechanism to strongly implement and support the State's educational goals. Led by the Minister of Education, school inspectors, as central government officials, were allocated by the Ministry of Education and they supervised mayors and school committees strictly in order to promote educational administration not as local and autonomous, but as a state's tasks. From this period, education was accelerated for the intensification of the Emperor System and national integration through nurturing morality and a spirit of patriotism and loyalty to the Emperor. Educational administration was regarded as a clerical task for the state to strongly supervise in order to realize and strengthen the governability. It is incorporated into a part of the general administration through the delegation to municipalities and becomes a so-called agency delegated function. With such a system, education oversight belonged to the Ministry of Home Affairs.

(3) Decentralization in postwar reform

After being defeated in the War in 1945, Japan started to completely reform the pre-war national education system based on deep reflections of that system, and by accepting instructions from the General Headquarters, the Supreme Commander for the Allied Powers (GHQ). In the Report of the United States Education Mission to Japan, a drastic reform plan was proposed and the Japanese Educational Innovation Committee discussed it in depth. As a result, principles of educational administration were replaced by the following three

Chapter 10. Features of Educational Administration in Japan   173

points.

Firstly, the principle of democracy (popular control) became its base, and this principle made it clear that people decide the quality and the way of running education. Secondly, rather than centralized, it should be operated on the principle that local government should deal with educational autonomy. Thirdly, since general administration was likely to be affected by the power of the time and lacked professional knowledge of and experience in education, the newly provided system of educational administration should depend on local autonomy and be independent from general administration (independence from general administration and ensuring independence of educational administration).

The organization of educational administration also has significantly reformed along this direction. The conventional centralized system was abolished and the educational authority was delegated to the local government. The board of education was established in prefectures and municipalities as an organization independent from general administration and was expected to play a substantial role in the field of educational administration.

The foundation of these changes was prescribed by the Constitution and the Fundamental Law of Education (FLE). The latter was enacted in the course of postwar reform. Following the Constitution, the FLE promulgated in 1947 clearly stated that education should not be subject to unjust control and it has a direct responsibility to all the people of the nation. In Article 8 and 9, political and religious neutralities were also described, which prohibits bias towards specific parties and religious sects. These were introduced upon reflection on the fact that pre-war education was deeply distorted by pressures of nationalism.

On the other hand, as the central organization of educational administration, the power of the Ministry of Education was drastically reduced. The roles were restricted to just giving advice and guidance, not strict supervision and control like the pre-war system and had to respect the autonomy of local authorities. It was emphasized that any advice or guidance should be limited to technical and professional issues.

2. Features of Educational Administration in Recent Years
(1) Decentralized or centralized

From the overview on progress of educational administration up to the present day, some points could be indicated as features of the Japanese system.

The first point is whether the educational administration continues to operate as a decentralized system or not. Theoretically, this debate has not yet been settled. In fact, both features could be observed through the procedures and process of their performance. This mixed situation can be considered as one feature of modern Japanese educational administration.

Of course, the current educational administration is not centralized like the pre-war days. The post-war educational administration is based on the principle of guidance and advice from the central government rather than command and supervision. In the last twenty years, the movement towards decentralization has become active in administrative functions including education in general. Since the 1990s, the division of roles between the central and local governments has been reconsidered. For example, legal binding power on class size provided as a national standard and student-teacher ratio has been deregulated. One of the reports of the Central Council for Education (CCE) and Ministry of Education, Redesigning compulsory education, issued in 2005, redrew the decentralized structural outline dividing roles between the central government and local governments.

Upon recognizing the central and local education administrations are equal, it suggested that the central government should guarantee national minimum standards, such as academic ability and educational circumstance, and that local governments should autonomously undertake various educational practices by utilizing their own resources to find "local optima".

On the other hand, education is still a symbol of national integration, and is grasped by centralized power. In contrast with the decentralization trend, the

FLE was amended towards centralization and nationalism in 2006. The word *patriotism* had been treated delicately in Japan as holding negative connotations rooted in experiences of oppression inside and outside the nation before and during World War II. But when it was amended in the 2006, such wording appeared. Although there was prudence and opposition regarding its inclusion, a political solution took place regarding this amendment.

Another example of centralization relates to the setting of national minimum standards mentioned above. It seems that the decentralized outline redrawn in that report will increased the autonomy of local educational administrations by changing the basic structure from pre-regulated to a post-check pattern. But some criticize that it is a new style of re-centralization, so called the "evaluation state", as educational outcomes are strictly controlled by the central government.

In 2013, the Ministry of Education directed the Okinawa Prefectural Board of education to implement corrective action toward Taketomi Town's Board of education regarding the adoption of textbooks in the Yaeyama area in Okinawa. It also directly requested the Taketomi Town Board of education to improve the situation. This intervention brought wide controversy whether local autonomy of the local governments was infringed or not. It is extremely characteristic of the educational field in Japan that centralized and political intervention based on differences in values and ideology are more prominent than levels of academic achievement and practicality.

(2) Increased intervention by politicians rooted in public distrust of education

The second feature is how educational administration is affected by peoples' negative opinions against school and its education. This may be the same situation in other countries by and large. The centralized tendencies of political parties have often been observed in recent years and have become very influential in some cases. In other words, the increased intervention by politicians regarding education seems to depend on people's distrust and criticism on education. This circumstances can also be said to be one of the features of Japanese educational administration in recent years.

Successive Japanese prime ministers had been highly interested in education. Education is important in the light of not only aiming to complete the students' characters, but also influences the future of Japanese society such as economy and industry. However, it is far from a large-scale reform in a short time. Actually continuity of education is important, and no simple solution can be found to resolve any problems of education. Success or failure of a new policy will be judged in the future. Although politicians are willing to change education somehow, they are prevented from intervening in education by the institution and must abide by political neutrality and independence from the general administration, in addition to reasons mentioned above. Prime ministers have attempted to change education by creating an advisory committee directly controlled by them. The National Council on Education Reform (NCER) which lasted for four years from 1984 is one of the notable examples.

As of 2017, Prime Minister Abe has also enthusiasm about education. He has organized the Headquarters of Implementing Educational Revitalization in the Liberal Democratic Party and the Council for Revitalization of Education (CRE) as a committee which he can directly control. These two agencies have strongly proposed important educational policies, such as university entrance examination reform and the reform of the board of education system, limiting the influence of the CCE which should be the central organization deciding educational policy.

Politicians' intervention in education can be observed at the local level as well by governors and mayors. In Osaka, the prefectural governor and the municipal mayor have gradually intervened in education asking the municipal board of education to open the results of the national achievement test to the public. They have also asked board of education to implement a rigorous evaluation system for school teachers which may lead to dismissal.

Chapter 10. Features of Educational Administration in Japan   177

Their extreme actions which infringed on the autonomy of education are incomprehensible. Yet they continue to be widely supported by people with unpleasant school memories and a distrust of schools and teachers. Under these circumstances, it is much more essential to understand the people's real desire for education and to confront their opinions as much as possible to improve the quality of education.

(3) Ethos of educational administration reflected by the teachers' culture

Thirdly, despite the situations described above, public servants in the office of educational administration are working to do their best and their efforts contribute to the task of educational administration both in central and local governments.

On the other hand, teachers in Japan sometimes have been appraised to make any effort for students and this atmosphere has definitely been developed among them as well as in other countries. While there were few jobs for child care in the past, Japanese teachers have been expected to undertake children's mental and intellectual development and are also proud of their job.

The custom of regular transfers of personnel between schools and educational administration offices has a shared mutual understanding and reciprocity on both sides.

For example, some teachers are recruited from schools to the secretariat of a board of education, supervisors at the prefecture and municipal levels. The positions of leaders in local educational administration such as superintendents also are likely to be persons with teaching experience. As explained in Chapter 8, the office of the board of education works independently from general administrations such as prefectural and municipal offices. Of course, although it should be accepted that there is a certain limit, such an ethos can be a cultural climate which neutralizes influences and demands from political and economic powers to some extent. It enables educational administration to guarantee the children's right to education and to develop, and the local people's right to learn.

The Ministry of Education also has a climate to respect circumstances in and around schools. Likewise, although the number of people is limited, there are personnel exchanges between them. Some school teachers are appointed as senior specialist for curriculum in the Ministry of Education or the National Institute for Educational Policy Research. Teacher culture is shared nationwide including regional differences and penetrates central and local organizations of educational administration. They are supported by the course of study which is applied uniformly to all over the country, many educational books and magazines in the private sector, and their own spontaneous research organizations of teachers. This may be one of the factors which make it difficult to decide whether the educational administration in Japan is centralized or decentralized as compared with other countries.

The culture of these organizations has an intention to give top priority to students and their development and this climate is an advantage of Japanese educational administration. However, the developing distrust against schools and teachers has especially brought this close relation among them to be seriously criticized as an "educational policy community" isolated from other areas just to protect their interests.

3. Perspective of Challenges and Features in Educational Administration

Today, Japan has to realize educational administration with new features that can respond to various social changes and educational challenges like other advanced industrialized countries. It is expected that the way will not be easy and that the future is filled with uncertainty and obscurity.

Of main importance is to secure and maintain a budget for public education under the condition of gradual decrease in the central government's revenue caused by economic stagnation in recent years.

The major expenditure of the education budget is personnel expenses such as teacher salaries. But it is difficult to reduce them, because their working condition directly affects to the quality of education. Especially teacher exhaustion due to over working has become very serious. This situation should be resolved by introducing effective policies, budget, and legislation to secure the quality of education as much as possible.

On the other hand in Japan, the declining birth rate and increase in the aging population have become serious problems with regards to public finance. Social needs for increased expenditure on welfare for the elderly are urgent and as a result, the expenditure for children's care and education has become a lower priority. Nonetheless, there are new and strong needs such as the enhancement of preschool education and care, and free higher education. Also, there is widespread public opinion to keep the current total number of teachers and much more so to decrease class size. These opinions can be drawn from the intension to raise the quality of education, and they oppose the general policy that decreasing the number of teachers should be a natural result of the declining birth rate. Based on these backgrounds, a discussion has been started on new ways of increasing financial resources such as educational government bonds and public children's care insurance in the National Diet, but it is hard to anticipate how they will turn out.

Secondly, administrative responsibility and/or accountability of education have become important. In other words, the relation between their competence at solving problems and their high-handed power, as well as the relation between politics and education are being discussed. As accountability has been strongly required, their problem solving competence is always questioned. As described above, the Prime Minister in the central government, and governors and mayors in the local government have strengthened their voices and are vigorously pressuring for reforms on schools and educational administration.

Initiatives and the leading of policies by the Prime Minister, governors and mayors seem attractive, because they can integrate and collaborate with a variety of social services for children such as welfare, medical care, juvenile justice, education and other human care, all of which are needed in order to handle the diverse, complicated and serious challenges that students and their families bring to school. On the contrary, schools and educational administration often tend to refuse such policies, because they are afraid that the Prime Minister, governors and mayors would not fully understand the complexity and difficulty of the tasks of education and would disturb the dignity and pride of the staff concerned.

Japan at present is faced with so many problems; how education keeps its relation to politics at a proper distance, how to collaborate with other fields as to human care services, and how to maintain the autonomy of educational administration and schools. All of them are quite complicated and answers are not so easy to find in a short time.

The third issue is to secure qualified staff with increased knowledge and skills of educational administration. It is also urgent to develop the professional ability among the present staff. Although educational administration expertise has not been recognized as essential to undertake their duties, schools as well as local offices of educational administration have to face quite serious problems which no one has ever experienced.

Central government officials are recruited mainly from the candidates who passed the examination for national public servants. They are appointed as general officials and are not required to have academic knowledge or a background in education and its administration. In one local board of education, the staff consists of both supervisors recruited from current teachers and general administrative officials who come from and soon return to the city office. Almost all of them are temporary transfers and usually do not have a high sense of belonging to educational administration.

Even if staff with teaching experience respects the educational practice itself, they do not necessarily have interest, hope, and motivation for educational administration. Expertise or professional knowledge and skills are acquired only after their appointment. They regularly ask to transfer to another department. It is uncertain whether knowledge and skills will remain after they leave. Furthermore, former teachers often wish to go back to schools and officials often wish to go back to other leading and active sections in a city office.

It was planned that the training and qualification system just for educational administrative experts was going to be established as a social system immediately after the World War II. But now, it is rare for such a system to be discussed, except for attempts at some universities.

Educational administration must be sophisticated and upgraded for raising the quality of education to innovate society according to various needs. Caught in a dilemma between criticism from society and pressure from politicians, it has become increasingly important for educational administration in Japan to play a highly recognized role and its officials are desired to become experts with professional knowledge.

Part 3

Movement for Reform

Chapter 11. Reform of Compulsory Education

1. Background of Reforms in Compulsory Education

Japan's compulsory education system is facing a period of great transformation through such measures as the revision of the School Education Law (SEL) in 2015 which institutionalized Compulsory education Schools. The underlying factors behind such measures are many difficulties and problems that the compulsory education system has exposed, that is, educational pathology. Reforms in compulsory education have been carried out to address such pathologies and some of the most representative issues are summarized below.

(1) Increase of absenteeism

A representative issue in educational pathology is the increase in school absenteeism. In 2014, the number of absenteeism (over 30 days a year) at the primary school level was approximately 26,000 students (an increase of 2000 from the previous year). At the lower secondary school level, the number was approximately 97,000 students (an increase of 2000 from the previous year). This means a ratio of 1 in 255 students at the primary school level and 1 in every 18 students at the lower secondary school level. Many students who become chronically absent already show such tendencies in primary school. Student guidance and family support are usually left entirely up to a single homeroom teacher leaving a more long-term system of continuous guidance from primary through lower secondary school desirable.

Although the reasons for absenteeism are diverse, two factors are the non-continuation of student guidance and course instruction from primary to lower secondary school which may lead to confusion and anxiety for many students. Thus, a system that takes into account the uniqueness of both primary and lower secondary schools while maintaining continuity in instruction and guidance is strongly desired.

(2) Earlier child development (Early maturation)

About 70 years have passed since the current 6-3 system was institutionalized and, during this time, there has been a remarkable acceleration of child development with marked increases in height and weight for 10-11 year olds and reports of the decline in the age of first menstruation in girls, indicating the earlier onset of puberty for upper grade primary school students. The characteristic traits of puberty are pointed out to be an increase in self-conscious, sensitivity to how one is viewed or judged by others, and high fluctuations in personality and emotions. However, the single-teacher-per-class system (in which one teacher is tasked with all instruction and student guidance) is still mainly used even for upper primary grades. Thus, there are many cases in which absenteeism or a complete collapse of classroom order occurs when students cannot form a good relationship with their homeroom teacher. This not only requires the urgent implementation of a specialist-teacher system for upper primary grades but also the cooperation of lower secondary school teachers.

(3) Widening academic achievement gap

Research by sociologists has also confirmed a widening gap in academic achievement among primary and lower secondary school students and the biggest factor is the widening gap in family income. It goes without saying that measures such as establishing a School Management Council to strengthen cooperation between communities and schools as well as improving overall welfare and labor policies are important. However, there are still many more issues that schools must address. All primary and lower secondary school teachers should share information on the degree of academic achievement required at the end of grade 9 which is the final stage of compulsory education as well as grasp when and why lower secondary school students fail in learning in order to teach more effectively. To realize this, primary and lower secondary school teachers should observe each other's classes and understand the structure and arrangement of instruction for each unit of study and how they relate to each other in order to improve their teaching methods.

(4) Consolidation and integration of schools

In today's Japan, there has been a drastic decline in the population of mountainous area communities, leading to a rise in extremely small-scale primary and lower secondary schools. In urban areas, the "doughnut effect" of city centers has worsened and many local communities have had to downsize. At the same time, in small municipalities, school buildings built during rapid population growth have reached the stage where they need to be rebuilt. However, without the necessary funds, they are forced to integrate with other school districts. This is why, in small municipalities, we often see cases where an extremely downsized primary school A is integrated with primary school B, the lower secondary school is rebuilt and the schools are all integrated into one facility. Compulsory Education Schools institutionalized with the amendment of the SEL in 2015 and unified primary & lower secondary schools have taken advantage of the difficulties of downsized schools facing closure to promote the new concept of continuous education from primary through lower secondary school.

2. Unified Primary & Lower Secondary School Education as a Tangible Reform in Compulsory Education
(1) Positive outcomes and challenges of unified primary & lower secondary school education according to a MEXT survey

According to a nationwide survey conducted by MEXT in 2014, out of 1743 municipalities town and village boards of education, 78% responded that they implemented unified or collaborative primary & lower secondary school education. These take several forms, i.e., integrated facilities, adjacent facilities or separate facilities.

The MEXT survey has indicated the following results:
1. The longer the engagement, the more positive outcomes achieved.
2. Implementation of a specialist-teacher system resulted in more positive outcomes.
3. Interactive "nori-ire" classes (where primary & lower secondary school teachers teach their specialized subjects at other's schools) showed more positive outcomes.
4. A one-principal management system for both schools showed more positive outcomes.
5. Compared to the present 6-3 system, the adoption of a different structure, particularly the 4-3-2 system, showed more positive outcomes.
6. Establishing 9-year educational goals and a 9-year curriculum schedule for each subject showed more positive outcomes.
7. Facilities adjacent to each other showed more positive outcomes than separate facilities and integrated facilities showed more positive outcomes than adjacent facilities.

The above results were an important factor in the amendment of the SEL in 2015 which institutionalized Compulsory Education Schools.

(2) 2014 Report of the central education council regarding unified primary & lower secondary school education

Compulsory education Schools were institutionalized by amendment of the SEL in June 2015. An important factor leading to this revision was the Report of the Central Council for Education (CCE) on December 22nd, 2014. This Report was based on results of a national survey in May 2014 by MEXT on unified primary and lower secondary school education as well as the 5th Proposal of the Council for Revitalization of Education (CRE) in July 2014. Chapter 1 entitled, "Institutionalization and comprehensive promotion of unified primary & lower secondary school education" is summarized below:

First, the background efforts in implementing unified primary & lower secondary school education are the repeal of a prescribed term for compulsory education by amendment of the FLE in 2006 and establishing provisions for new objectives and aims in compulsory education by amendment of the SEL in 2007. An increase in such issues in compulsory education as earlier development (maturation) of students, absenteeism after entering lower secondary school, the problem of bullying, and an increase in extremely small-scale schools has become apparent and measures to address these issues are strongly desired.

Also, according to a national survey, most schools that have implemented unified primary & lower secondary school education have shown many positive outcomes such as improved student academic achievement, alleviation of the "grade 7-gap" (i.e., anxieties associated with entering lower secondary school), and heightened awareness and improved leadership skills of the teaching staff. However, relieving the workload of the teaching staff remains an issue that needs to be resolved.

The basic direction and objectives of system design for unified primary & secondary school education are to establish new schools which are able to design a well-organized, coherent 9-year curriculum based on an integrated organizational structure. When it has been determined that a unified primary & lower secondary school is valid by taking the conditions and circumstances of the local community into consideration, an environment should be created in which such a school can be smoothly and effectively established. Such efforts are also expected to promote the nationwide implementation of excellent unified primary & lower secondary school education as well as enhance cooperation between existing primary and lower secondary schools in order to improve the overall quality of compulsory education.

3. Compulsory Education Schools & Unified Primary & Lower Secondary Schools

(1) Regulations and conditions for establishing a school

Amendment of the SEL in June 2015 and subsequent revisions to government ordinances have institutionalized Compulsory Education Schools and unified primary & lower secondary schools (referred to as an integrated primary & lower secondary school when the founder is the same or collaborative primary & lower secondary school when the founder is different), as shown in **Table 11-1**.

Table 11-1 Compulsory Education Schools

Length of study	9 years of study (however, to facilitate smooth transfers between schools, this has been divided into 6 years for the 1st stage and 3 years for the latter stage).
Curriculum	Establishing a 9-year educational goal and the design of a comprehensive curriculum based on a 9-year system.
	Upon preparation of curriculum guidelines for primary & lower secondary schools, special exceptions and guidelines to implement unified education can also be established (e.g. design of new courses and replacement or expansion of instruction guidelines).
Organization	One principal, one faculty & staff organization. In principle, both primary & lower secondary school teaching licenses are required.
Facilities & Equipment	Can be installed regardless of whether the schools are integrated or separate.

Prior to the Ordinance for Enforcement of the SEL in April 2016, MEXT conducted a survey in February 2016 of prefectural and municipality, and town and village boards of education regarding the introduction of Compulsory Education Schools and unified primary & lower secondary schools. According to this survey, 136 public Compulsory Education Schools are planned and, as of April 2016, 22 have opened. Among the 13 prefectures and 15 municipalities, towns and villages, a high number of schools, 109 (80%), are integrated facilities.

(2) Future issues and challenges

An original curriculum based on the needs of the local community and actual situation of the children can be designed by the founder of newly institutionalized Compulsory Education Schools and unified primary & lower secondary schools without approval for special curricular guidelines & exceptions or designation as a research & development school. However, in reality, an original and different curriculum cannot be realized when relying only on the guidance and advice of individual schools or municipality, or town and village boards of education. Many municipalities have established an education center. However, these are overburdened with consulting work and are not able to provide the guidance and advice necessary to assist in the design of an appropriate original curriculum. Proactive and useful guidance and advice from prefectural boards of education to municipality, town and village boards of education are strongly desired. Cases of progressive efforts across the country should be introduced and sending teaching staff to such schools as observers would also be effective. Since the late 1990's, decentralization has, in principle, given municipalities, towns and villages more autonomy and independence. However, this has also led to the biggest problem of relegating tasks concerning compulsory education exclusively to local governments.

Column-9: Absenteeism and Free School

In Japan, more than 120,000 primary and lower secondary school students are absent from school for over 30 days for reasons other than illness or poverty. Although many people regarded these students as just lazy, the MESSC at that time acknowledged that absenteeism was a phenomenon that could occur in any child and be caused by the troubles of school life such as bullying, academic underachievement, and a feeling of distrust of teachers. Subsequently, MEXT has again urged them to attend school by promoting the distribution of school counselors and the establishment of adaptation classes. However, the number of students who refuse to attend school has not decrease.

To address the circumstances surrounding absenteeism, the practice of alternative education called "free school" has received a lot of attention in recent years. Free schools were founded to take in students who refused to attend school even before the MESSC acknowledged it. Since some of the free schools adopted a confrontational approach to public education and criticized the uniformity of public schools, local governments did not give a favorable response to their practice. However, some local governments have attempted to give subsidies and official certification to free schools in recent years. In 2015, MEXT set up "Council for Free Schools", which deliberated on the learning and monetary support system to the children using free schools. In addition, the law on the securement of educational opportunity for those students was enacted in 2016.

The number of local governments which attempt to collaborate with free schools may increase. However, some researchers express concern about the danger of free schools losing their uniqueness as a result of regulations that the local governments may impose in exchange for subsidies. We need to pay particular attention to how free schools are affected by being benefactors of government subsidies and receiving official certification.

Chapter 12. Secondary Education Reforms

1. Issues Faced
(1) Lower secondary education

Secondary education consists of lower and upper secondary education, and the former is regarded as a second half of compulsory education. However, there are significant differences between them. For instance, teachers in primary schools are in charge of whole subjects of one class while lower secondary schools teachers are mainly subject-based. As to the atmosphere, lower secondary schools impose a lot of rules on students compared to primary schools and tend to enforce them strictly. Also students at this age have to face significant physical growth, become interested in sexual matters, and are also very unstable both physically and mentally. In this situation, they have to prepare for upper secondary school entrance examinations and their surroundings are very much complicated. Bullying and absenteeism happen much more in lower secondary school than primary school.

(2) Upper secondary education

98% of lower secondary school students continue to upper secondary school and as a result, their interests, abilities, aptitudes and future courses differ from each other and also they have a variety of demands and expectations. Under these circumstances, various types of schools have been established (Refer to Section 3 of Chapter 1, Part I) and school reforms (such as expansion of schools' discretion) have taken place. However, gaps in academic achievement among students have become more serious within individual schools as well as in the system as a whole. The most important issue regarding Japan's upper secondary school education is how to ensure the quality of education while maintaining balance between "assurance of commonality" and "responses towards diversification". In addition, the ratio of enrollment in upper secondary schools is high while there are also some students who did not attend school for a long time or were sometimes absent. They numbered approximately 1.4% of the total number of students (according to the "survey on issues regarding student guidance concerning student's behavior problems" conducted in 2015). Meanwhile, there have been poor policies for students with special needs

2. Secondary Education Reforms
(1) Extra-curricular cubs

While teachers in other countries mainly focus on giving lessons, teachers in Japan are expected to undertake various tasks such as giving lessons, student guidance, and counselling and supervision of extra-curricular club activities.

Extra-curricular club activities are flourishing in each school under the initiative and guidance of concerned persons including teachers who serve as advisors. About 90% of students belong to a club as shown in **Fig.12-1**.

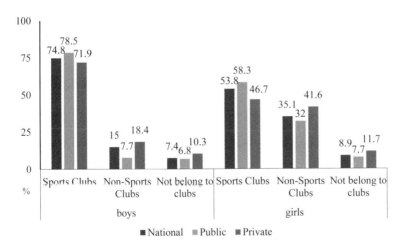

Fig. 12-1 Ratio of Students belonging to Extra-curricular Clubs, 2016

(Prepared based on the Results of the "*National Survey on the Physical Strength and Athletic Ability* (Japan Sports Agency)", 2016.)

Although such activities are highly significant in terms of educational aspects, excessive activities bring negative effects. In particular, some teachers are overloaded with work and about half of lower secondary school teachers feel stressed due to extra-curricular club responsibilities. To resolve this situation, MEXT and the Japan Sports Agency recently required schools to reduce their burdens.

(2) Coexistence of private and public schools

Unified lower and upper secondary school education which used to be dominant among the private sector, has been rapidly increasing recently among publicly provided schools **(Fig.12-2)**. This trend will bring a fair competition between them.

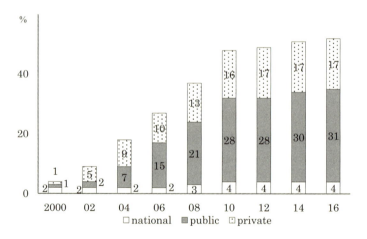

Fig. 12-2 Number of Secondary Education Schools

(Prepared based on MEXT *"School Basic Research: Annual Statistics"*)

In the Report of the Council for Regulation Reform (2008), it required that private and public schools shall compete with each other on equal terms by giving special considerations from the perspective of prosperous coexistence and proposed to let both types of schools have opportunities to discuss the candidate selection process and effective school management.

(3) Unified lower and upper secondary school education

After the Report by the Central Council for Education (CCE, 1997), the unified junior and upper secondary school education system was introduced in 1999 in order to promote the diversification of secondary education and to realize a continuous six-year education with an integrated curriculum and learning environment. The education reform program (by MEXT) expected about 500 schools nation widely.

The total number of such schools was 595 (National: 5, Publicly provided: 194, Private: 396) in 2015 and the target number of 500 seems to have been achieved. As private schools hold 66.6% and the number of such schools has increased particularly in urban areas, this new policy has not been realized successfully in the public sector.

These unified schools consist of three patterns. Firstly, the school is organized as just one with six grades. Secondly, in the case of a lower and upper secondary school established by the same founder, students can proceed to the latter without undergoing any selective procedures. The third is a collaboration type. In this case, separate lower and upper secondary schools co-develop education as well as curriculums, and collaborate on teacher and student exchanges.

Schools of second pattern are located in urban areas, while the third type is found in rural districts and play a role in local development as a community school.

The main advantages of this school are indicated in a governmental report that (1) students can spend a relaxed and stable school life without high school entrance examinations, (2) six-year education plans can be continuously carried out, (3) it becomes easier to develop students' individualities and discover their abilities, and (4) students' sociality and rich humanity are developed through various activities with different aged students.

On the other hand, the main problems were also pointed out (1) the younger children are involved in competitive entrance examinations, (2) an education overly biased toward entrance examinations may be provided, (3) it is difficult to find future possibilities after leaving primary school, and (4) problems may arise when members of intimate group are fixed for a long time. Actually, such advantages and problems have been recognized already and some schools are very proud of having excellent entrance exam results for leading universities. On the contrary, some students become lazy and the academic gap can be clearly recognized. However, this reform of two different schools being integrated could be recognized as providing effective education and expanding a range of choices available to students and parents.

Pic.12-1 The First Secondary School

(This school was established for the first time in 1994 combining a lower and upper secondary school on the same campus.)

(4) Academic achievement gaps

There are significant gaps as to the academic achievements among students in upper secondary education. Furthermore, gaps in motivation towards learning are admitted to be wider. Each school tries to enhance student motivation in

Chapter 12. Secondary Education Reforms   197

their own ways such as the formation of curriculums in accordance with students' actual situations, and giving lessons in small groups or in accordance with their academic abilities. Each school needs to pursue ways to develop the individualities and abilities of each student by taking actual situations of districts and students into consideration. Two characteristic types of upper secondary school education shown below could be examples to resolve this serious problem.

(5) Tuition-free in upper secondary school

There is a clear connection between students' academic achievement and their socio-economic background. Many municipalities actively provide financial support for compulsory education in disadvantaged districts.

Average of tuition fee of one year for upper secondary school (day course) is 118,000 yen (US$ 1,072) for publicly provided schools and 390,578 yen (US$ 3,545) for private schools according to a 2015 MEXT survey. Other expenses, such as for commuting, learning materials and extra-curricular activities, are much higher than compulsory education. There are many cases where students are obliged not to be enrolled in upper secondary schools or drop out of the schools after enrollment because of financial difficulties.

A new system was introduced in 2014 to support for upper secondary school students depending on students' household income. Under this system, grants for financial support for upper secondary school students are provided for those whose household income is less than around 9.1 million yen (US$ 83 thousand) in a year. Some local governments like Osaka Prefecture expanded the system and adopted a substantially reduced or tuition-free policy for private upper secondary schools.

It has been pointed out that the policy was going to promote equal opportunities for education and to increase competition between publicly provided and private schools regardless of the financial burden placed on parents.

3. Issues that Secondary Education faces in the Future

The international competition of human resources has grown sharper because of globalization, rapid progress of science and technology as well as diversity of values in a changing society. In other words, society needs various abilities which accord to the complicated social structure which changes frequently. In this context, issues regarding secondary education will increase more than ever and also, education should be delivered to respond to each student properly. The major roles of secondary education should accurately correspond to the changing society and should secure and improve its quality. Additionally, the working condition of teaching staff should be improved to realize these targets.

Column-10: Career Education

In the 1990's, the increase in the number of part-time workers became serious, and MEXT proposed career education for students to improve attitudes to work and vocational abilities. It was accepted in a short time because youth employment was so serious, triggered by the structural change of industries, resolution by the central government was needed. For the younger generation work experience and on the job training are regarded as important to promote self-sufficiency and cooperation among ministries, industries, schools and local communities have developed so far.

Today, life career is changing according to the diversity of working styles and career education is intended to nurture independence not only for jobs, but also sound citizens. In 2011, the Central Council for Education (CCE) reported that career education means to promote "career development to actualize way of life while playing a role in society" and to "develop basic abilities and attitudes for social and occupational independence". Those abilities include good human relations, to build society and to solve problems. For this purpose, such education could be done through subjects and activities in school curriculum. Every school is prompted to have an original yearly plan, but any problems are left out for its evaluation.

In primary school, they set to develop the feeling of responsibility and self-esteem through committee activities. They visit places concerning jobs for their daily life as social studies trips and participate in regional exchanges with the local people. In lower secondary school, there are work experience, volunteer activities, and the other opportunities to learn. Students are expected to think about how to live and work to enhance their sense of purpose for learning. In upper secondary school, lectures by working adults, activities in companies and internships are provided for students to examine their own abilities to plan for their future after leaving school. In higher education, lectures on career, support for employment and internship are provided.

Chapter 13. Higher Education Reform

1. Connection between Upper Secondary School and Higher Education
(1) University entrance examination

The ratio of students who go on to higher education has been increasing steadily and reached about 60% in recent years, under the social atmosphere and changes in social and economic structures followed by the transition to a modern society. Additionally, students with various academic performance, talent, and motivation are likely to continue on to higher education. A serious problem in universities, which are not so strict in terms of selection intensity, is that there are many students whose ability to think, judge, and express themselves, as well as their basic knowledge, and skills are not enough.

To solve these problems of disconnect between upper secondary school and higher education, the MEXT of Japan has made various proposals regarding system reform. Especially, it is worthy to notice that the Central Council for Education (CCE) made a report titled "About the Integral Revolution of Upper Secondary School Education, Higher Education, and Higher Education Entrance Examination to Realize Connection between Upper Secondary School and Higher Education Suited for New Era" ("Connection Report") in December 2014. The "Connection Report" presented the basic position that it is important to select entrants of higher education, bearing in mind a "zest for living" and "solid academic ability". Based on this, the "Connection Report" suggested the following plan about higher education entrance examination.

Firstly, it proposed the abolition of the current National Center Test for University Admission (NCTUA). It has played an important role in securing basic academic skills for upper secondary school students as a whole, in addition to its original role as a judge of the degree of basic academic skill achieved by applicants. On the other hand, it has focused on only "knowledge and skills" of "solid academic ability" and it has failed to properly measure possible academic performance of students at the higher education stage. So, the "Connection

Report" suggested the abolition of it and a new method is to replace it in the near future.

This new type of exam is called "test of estimation of school achievements for applicants". This test aims to measure the ability necessary for higher education. It is to evaluate not only "knowledge and skills" of "solid academic ability" independently, but also the "ability to think, judge, and express which is necessary for making knowledge and skills more active, for example, discovering problems, inquiring about solutions, and presenting the process and its outcome". The features of this test are as follows; (1) to provide questions that "cover a few subjects" and, to evaluate ones "ability to think, judge, and express" beyond the limit of current subjects, in addition to evaluate ability of the "type of subject", (2) to introduce not only multiple choice type questions, but also narrative questions, (3) to give a challenging chance to applicants, and conduct entrance examinations several times a year to promote the effectiveness of the qualification test, (4) to provide higher education institutes and applicants test results presented by grades from the point of view of promoting the introduction of various evaluation methods in each university's entrance examination.

Thirdly, it asked universities to improve their own entrance examinations. About this examination, the CCE suggested various types of questions based on the three elements of "solid academic ability". On top of that, to promote students with various backgrounds, the Council insisted that each university defined their selective procedure to be able to meet its admission policy, education and so on. It is anticipated that this definition clearly presented how to evaluate the various abilities students should acquire at the upper secondary school stage of education.

(2) Cooperation between upper secondary school and university

In recent years, the relation between upper secondary schools and universities has come into focus. One of the aspects is to just give opportunities for upper secondary school students to experience the higher education stage. The main programs of this cooperation are as follows; lectures by faculty of higher education institutes which take place at upper secondary schools, extension lectures which are targeted at upper secondary school students, completion of regular university lectures for upper secondary school students and open campus. At present, upper secondary schools certify upper secondary school student's completion of lectures at university as upper secondary school credit. In the future, it is expected that these programs will expand, and furthermore closer communications between them will be developed in the near future.

(3) Expansion of first year experience

Under the present circumstances of higher education with various kinds of students, the first year experience program has been introduced gradually so they can adjust to their new life very smoothly. The programs of first-year-experience are provided according to the differences and needs of students. The methods of how to write report, presentation skills, Information and Communication Technology (ICT) skills, hot to conduct field work, surveys, and experiences, methods of collecting information and material arrangement, critical thinking, finding problems and how to solve them intellectually, motivation for study and overall higher education, motivation for future working life and career path selection, awareness and feeling of responsibility as a social constituent, time management, study habits and so on.

2. Procedures and Methods of Higher Education
(1) Suggestion by "Qualitative Change Report"

The MEXT of Japan has made many proposals about regarding higher education. In these proposals, it is worth noticing that the CCE made a report "Toward the Qualitative Change of Higher Education to Build New Future." ("Qualitative Change Report") in August 2012. This report pointed out that our society has been changing and accordingly, it has brought doubt on the standard of common sense under rapid globalization, the decreasing birth rate and on the contrary, the increasing elderly population, the energy and food crisis, and regional disparity. Then, the "Qualitative Change Report" pointed out the importance of the ability to find and solve problems with proper procedures, the needs of life-long learning depending on personal interests etc.

As the starting point, it recognizes the function of education to enrich the quality of individual life. In this context it showed the meaning and necessity of initiative learning time. Then, it also suggested that student needs to learn how to study independently and faculty has to improve educational programs and methods to prompt a student's independent learning. As a whole, university itself is asked to promote and support the needs to insure such faculty's effort. In another word, this report should be accepted to make the curriculum of each faculty systematic and to accelerate the implementation of an integrated and refined educational program and also to provide a sufficient syllabus. These efforts will bring the implementation of organizational education, fullness of syllabus, and establishment of overall education and learning management. We will take up these hereafter.

(2) Systematic curriculum

First of all, this report asks to show the educational outline which the university is going to provide as a whole. For example, they show the target of learning in each faculty or department and positive relations of different classes to each other. It indicates universities need to easily present structure of curriculum, such as numbering relations between lectures, program difficulty to make students and persons concerned to understand curriculum system easier. To promote these efforts, "Qualitative Change Report" pointed out that preparation of a diploma policy as well as a curriculum policy and admission policy become much more important than ever. The research undertaken by the MEXT of Japan in 2013 showed that preparation ratios of these policies are approximately 94%, 94% and 97% respectively. Meanwhile, ratio of consistency between diploma policy etc. and curriculum is about 74%, so this is still a major problem to be solved.

(3) Implementation of organizational education

Implementation of organizational education in each faculty, based on the above systematic curriculum is also important. Previously, there has been a tendency that each faculty is responsible for lectures and their class management and they also set their own targets. However, for qualitative change, they have been asked to improve it. In addition to a systematic curriculum created by independent engagement of the whole faculty, the following two points may be important to realize organizational education.

Firstly, it is important to introduce the active learning process through which students independently seek to discover and solve problems with various people. The team work activities with a small group, group discussion, flipped classrooms, studying abroad, and internship would be recommended.

Secondly, it is also important to improve the evaluation of student learning outcomes, focusing on what they actually learned. For example, there are system developments for exact records of learning process and self-evaluation, developments for grasping learning outcomes and evaluation methods making use of test and investigation of learned behavior, and implementing strict grading and graduation approval, on the assumption that the university has adopted a common assessment policy at large.

The research made by the MEXT of Japan in 2013 shows that the number of universities which consider introducing active learning into curriculum increased from 407 universities (55%) in 2012 to 454 universities (62%) in 2013. This result also shows that the number of universities which can precisely see the situation of students learning increased from 299 universities (40%) in 2012 to 441 universities (60%) in 2013. Furthermore, the number of universities which show student learning outcomes through curriculum increased from 265 universities (36%) in 2012 to 345 universities (47%) in 2013.

(4) Fullness of syllabus

"Qualitative Change Report" indicates that the syllabus does not merely show a simple overview of lecture, but enables students to actively prepare for and review lectures. Also it is expected to be used as a road map of raising the quality of the class.

(5) Providing total management system

"Qualitative Change Report" indicates that universities should establish overall education and learning management, and proceed with reform cycles about higher education to discover and solve various problems including improvement of education skills. It requires the development of management and business minds among university staff to succeed in education and learning management. In this context, faculty development was obligated in April 2008. On the other hand, research made by the MEXT of Japan in 2013 shows that the number of universities which implemented staff development was limited to 31%. But, since staff development was obligated in April 2016, it is anticipated that in-service training for staff will be developed much more than before. Furthermore, we can see some universities implement training programs for graduate students who are expected to be academic staff in the near future.

3. React to Globalization, and Decreasing Birth Rate and Aging Population

In recent years, international competition between universities has stood out to accept students from abroad and to develop the highest level research and education in the world. However, because of the decreasing birth rate and increase in the elderly population on the contrary, university enrollment has decreased. Furthermore, there are some universities which are finding it difficult to meet their new student quota and in some cases, are facing a survival crisis. To resolve these serious problems, universities are required to undertake various reforms. In June 2013, "The Basic Plan for Promoting Education" suggested functional enhancement of university governance and a policy to increase the number of students from abroad.

Firstly, it pointed out functional enhancement of university governance. The Basic Plan indicated the importance of an effective governance structure, one which the president of the university can utilize his strong leadership to bring out each faculty's motivation and the talent of individual academic staff from all fields in the university. In response to this, the Ordinance for Enforcement for the SEL was revised to strengthen the authority of university presidents in April 2015. To be more specific, system reform such as making the vice president's role more powerful and the function of faculty meeting less powerful than before. It states the vice president can undertake his duty as to university management within the range of the president's direction to strengthen the president's assistance system. About faculty meetings, it was provided that faculty meetings are an organization which discusses its education and research, and could only give proposals or opinions to the president who holds any final decisions.

Yet, about the governance of national universities, it was reorganized as a national university corporation in April 2004. The purpose of this policy was to develop an increased competitive potential among them, and in fact, financial freedom was approved in spite of their income being expended by the central government. Also, by the extension of discretion in personnel, the status of all academic staff can be changed to the non-civil servant type. As such circumstances of further globalization, decreasing birth rate, and the increase in the elderly population have become serious, national university corporation is proceeding with various reforms to have competitive power and to establish a self-improvement and self-development system since April 2016.

Secondly, it is to promote the policy to increase the number of overseas students who study in Japan. It has been lower than other advanced countries. The MEXT of Japan and other relevant government offices released "The Plan of 300,000 Overseas Students" in July 2008, and set the goal of accepting 300,000 overseas students by 2020. The Cabinet Office established an "Active Plan of Promoting Youth Studying Abroad" in April 2014. This office adjusts the system and strengthens its effect on the industrial world and universities to attain the goal of increasing the number of students studying abroad from 60,000 to 120,000 by 2020.

Chapter 14. Internationalization of Education

1. Internationalization of School Education
(1) Education for children living abroad with the intent to return to Japan

Since the high economic growth period of the 1960s, Japanese companies have been actively expanding their business abroad and the number of school age children accompanying their parents to live in foreign countries has been increasing year by year.

According to data from the MEXT, there were approximately 78,000 Japanese children of compulsory education age living in foreign countries in 2015. And in 2014, approximately 12,000 children returned to Japan after living abroad for a considerable time span. As for overseas educational institutions, there are full-time schools for Japanese citizens and supplementary education schools for part-time Japanese education. Full-time schools for Japanese citizens are educational institutions for Japanese children living overseas which are equivalent to domestic primary, lower and upper secondary schools, and are certified by the Minister of MEXT. Supplementary education schools are educational institutions which conduct classes in Japanese for some subjects on Saturdays and after school. There were 89 full-time schools for Japanese citizens and 205 supplementary education schools throughout the world in 2015.

Looking at the number of students in each school in 2015, 20,615 children (26.3%) attended full-time schools for Japanese, 19,894 children (25.4%) attended supplementary education schools and local schools and 37,803 children (48.3%) attended local schools. As for regions, in the Asian region, a majority of Japanese children attended full-time schools. Whereas in the North American and European region, a majority of Japanese children attended local schools and supplementary education schools.

(2) Education for foreign children in Japan

The total number of foreign children in Japan was 73,289 in 2014. According to school age, there were 42,721 children attending primary schools, 21,143 children attending lower secondary schools, 8,584 children attending upper secondary schools, 211 children in secondary schools and 630 children attending special needs schools. Of the total number, 29,198 needed Japanese language instruction.

Fig. 14-1   The Number of Children who need Japanese Instruction

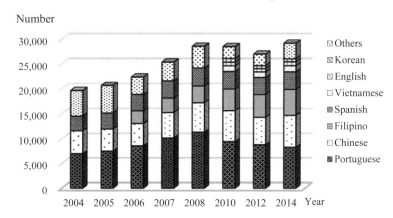

*The following languages have been added: since 2006, Filipino, since 2010, Vietnamese, English and Korean.   (MEXT, 2015)

As for the children's native languages, there were 8,340 Portuguese speaking children, 6,410 Chinese speaking children, 5,153 Filipino speaking children, 3,576 Spanish speaking children, 1,215 Vietnamese speaking children and so on in 2014 **(Fig.14-1)**. Foreign children who needed Japanese language instruction are mostly temporary stay newcomers. As for areas of residence, many newcomers live in large industrial areas. For example, 11,812 children (40.5%) live in the Tokai region and 10,081 children (34.5%) live in the Kanto region.

Native language education and education of their ethnic identity are rarely implemented for foreign children or children with foreign experience, while Japanese schools are implementing assimilative education with the aim of children being able to acquire Japanese language and Japanese culture. This educational method leads to a deprivation of the children's own cultures and identities. Even though there are children with different cultural backgrounds, Japanese schools promote assimilative education rather than trying to interact with different cultures and exposing Japanese students to them. Under such circumstances it cannot be said that internationalization of school education in Japan is proceeding.

(3) Foreign language education

In Japan, foreign language education has been conducted at lower and upper secondary schools for a long time, but the start time of foreign language education is later compared to other countries. Fifth and sixth grade children have been learning English as part of "foreign language activities" since 2010. Primary school English education is aimed at enhancing communication skills through activities with the aim that children become familiar with the spoken element of English. From 2020, foreign languages from 5th and 6th grade will be introduced as regular subjects, and 3rd and 4th grade children will commence compulsory "foreign language activities". In other words, there is a progression to strengthen foreign language education from the primary education stage.

One of the important problems of foreign language education in Japan is the foreign language which children can select, is mainly restricted to English. There were 708 upper secondary schools which offered foreign language subjects other than English in 2014. As for the languages offered, there were 517 schools (19,106 students) offered Chinese, 333 schools offered Korean (11,210 students), 223 schools offered French (9,214 students) and 107 schools offered German (3,691 students). The total number of upper secondary schools was a mere 4,963 schools, hence it can be said that there are only a few upper secondary school students learning foreign languages other than English. Primary school, lower and upper secondary school have hardly ever conducted foreign language education for languages other than English. In promoting international understanding and understanding of different cultures in the era of regionalization, the current situation shows that there is almost no opportunity for children to be exposed to Asian languages. Specializing only in English as a foreign language is a serious problem that needs to be addressed.

(4) Declining overseas orientation of young people

Japanese young people are losing interest in overseas and "introverted thinking" is progressing. While the number of young Chinese and Korean students studying abroad is increasing, the number of Japanese students is decreasing. According to OECD data, the number of Japanese students of post-secondary education, studying abroad was 15,246 in 1984, it increased more than 5 times over the next 20 years. However, it has declined since it peaked at 82,945 students in 2004 and decreased to 60,138 students in 2012. On the other hand, the number of Chinese and South Korean students has increased more than 1.5 times for the same time period.

The progression of a declining birth rate and the accompanying increase in the capacity of domestic universities to accommodate students is one of reasons why the number of young Japanese studying abroad has decreased. Since the latter half of the 2000s the capacity of domestic universities has exceeded 90%, and it is no longer necessary to go to foreign universities in this era being called "the era in which university places outnumber university applicants". In addition, the deterioration of household income due to the recession is another reason. Looking at the average income per household, income has decreased since the peak of 6.642 million yen (about 58 thousand US dollars) in 1994. In 2012, household income has decreased to 5.372 million yen (47 thousand US dollars).

212

2. Education for International Understanding

"Education for International Understanding" is an education "to develop basic attitudes and capacities required for acting positively with global perspectives in an international society"[13]. Recently, MEXT called it "International Education", however, the term "Education for International Understanding" is widely known in Japanese society.

(1) Summary of development

Development of Education for International Understanding could be classified in four stages. From 1946 to 1973, education for International Understanding had been explored with an aim of establishing peace stemming from regret over World War II. However it was not expanded widely in Japan.

In the 1970's, Japan's role in international society was recognized and "developing Japan living in an international society" had been set as an important policy in the report of the Central Council for Education (CCE) in 1974. As areas to assume this basic agenda, foreign language education, internationalization of universities and Education for International Understanding emerged. However, the center of the agenda was limited to education for Japanese children abroad and an increase of sending teachers abroad, etc. Development education aiming to enhance an understanding of poverty in developing countries and a gap between those and developed countries, etc. was not covered.

The 1980's was the stage when Education for International Understanding expanded. In 1985, the National Council on Education Reform (NCER) launched an educational reform policy in their first report with a view of "internationalization of Japan". Based on that, "deepening International Education and putting great value on developing attitudes to respect Japanese

---

13　MEXT, (2005) *Report of the Conference for Promoting International Education for the Primary and Lower Secondary Education: To Develop Human Resources living in the International Society* (in Japanese).

culture and tradition" were placed in the revised course of study in 1989. In each local board of education, urgency for promoting Education for International Understanding in educational instruction and school collaboration was prioritized. Training activities for teachers in charge and making guidelines, etc. also took place [14].

The late 1990's was an exponential turning point for Education for International Understanding. In the course of study of 1999, "period for integrated study" was newly added and Education for International Understanding was stipulated as an example for the integrated study which was epoch-making. The MEXT launched a policy to align education for Japanese children abroad, for those coming back from foreign countries and for foreign children and Education for International Understanding towards a direction of "International Education". The Ministry placed "International Education" as an education to lead to "zest for living", a basic principle of the existing course of study revised in 2008 to 2009. In the 2010's, Education for International Understanding became a concrete measure of the Ministry's new policy of the "development of global human resources". Furthermore, as a background to that "Education for Sustainable Development (ESD)", which is a close concept to Education for International Understanding and Development Education, was adopted by the United Nations in 2002, the Ministry has promoted ESD and took its view in the existing course of study. On the other hand, although Development Education has started to be introduced in extra-curricular activities in Japan, it is not as widely known or conducted yet compared to Education for International Understanding.

---

14   Minei. A. (2001). *'Education for International Education: Its Developments after the War and Current Issues'*. Amano, M. & Murata, Y. (Eds.), *Education in the Multicultural Society* (in Japanese). Tokyo: Tamagawa University Press.

(2) Implementation status and in-service teacher training of education for international understanding

Overall, Education for International Understanding is conducted in subjects such as social studies, living environment studies (grade 1 and 2) and Japanese language, as well as extra-curricular activities, moral education, and period for integrated study at each primary, lower and upper secondary school. In research conducted in 2015, among the above-mentioned cases, the percentage of public primary and lower secondary schools implementing Education for International Understanding in the period for integrated study is 60 percent and 40 percent respectively, although more recently, that percentage has declined. As for full-time public upper secondary school, about 40 percent of all general courses are conducting Education for International Understanding although the percentage varies among general courses, specialized vocational courses, and comprehensive courses.

As for contents, the percentage of traditional themes such as understanding different cultures, English language, and international exchanges, etc. tends to be high. On the other hand, the percentage of contents related to Development Education such as problems of poverty and conflicts is relatively low. As for learning methods, styles which are not held to existing whole class teaching such as investigative learning, use of audiovisual aids, exchanges with foreigners in Japan, and experience learning, etc. are being introduced.

(3) Challenges and perspectives

Education for International Understanding is in line with "zest for living", a basic principle of the existing course of study. However it is not a subject and its implementation status differs depending on school, teachers, and its contents are also limited. The following three challenges could be raised to respond to those situations.

First is an institutional challenge. In order to have Education for International Understanding becoming widespread, it could be useful to locate it clearly in the curriculum as well as in the in-service and pre-service training for teachers. In doing so, it is worth considering making contents related to Education for International Understanding as a subject like examples from other countries.

Second is a challenge of learning contents. From now on, Education for International Understanding with the perspective of a borderless and global society is needed. Therefore, it is important to create objectives and contents of the following four learning areas and implement them [15]. The first area is multicultural society. It is to learn understanding and tolerance of different cultures. Especially, Development Education for promoting understanding of such topics as poverty of developing countries is important. The second area is global society. It is important to promote understanding of global interdependency as global citizens. The third one is global issues, such as human rights, environment, peace and development and to promote understanding that ESD is a common important agenda for the entire world. The fourth is the area of choice for the future. Learning objectives include an understanding of history, public awareness, and participation and cooperation.

Finally, the third challenge is to develop teachers who are able to implement education for International Understanding, arrange the learning environment and use local human resources. It is hoped to create a structured curriculum of in-service training courses and implement them for teachers to enhance their practical teaching skills.

3. International Exchange and Cooperation

In order to internationalize education, the promotion of international education exchange and cooperation is also important. While the number of Japanese students going abroad to study is decreasing, the number of foreigners coming to Japan to study is increasing. The total number of foreign students

---

15　Japan Association for International Education. (2012). *Education for International Understanding in the Global Era: Connecting the Practice and Theory* (in Japanese), Tokyo, Akashi Shoten.

including those at universities, technical colleges, vocational schools, and Japanese language schools was 239,287 in May of 2016, a 15% increase compared to 2015.

As the number of foreign students is increasing, the system to accept them should be improved. Examples are to improve the counselling system for foreign students, to increase academic staff supervising them, and to promote teaching and educational activities for understanding different cultures and accepting them in Japanese society after their course graduation. As a result, there are many plans to increase dormitories for foreign students. This was also referred to in the government's plan to increase foreign students to 300,000 by 2020 which was announced in 2008. In the dormitories allocated to them, only foreign students, no Japanese students, lived there. From now it is necessary for Japanese students to live together with foreign students in order to deepen their understanding of different cultures and let them consider the coexistence of multi-cultures.

Concerning international education exchange, such programs in primary and secondary schools are conducted including overseas Japanese school students and foreign students in Japanese schools as well as universities. Although these enterprises are not so popular recently, upper secondary school students going abroad to study, including short term studies, have increased.

International education cooperation is also carried out in Japan. Many developing countries devise autonomous development of basic education. The Japanese government, local governments, and NGO's extend educational assistance in various forms to those programs such as school facilities, equipments, in-service training of their teachers, and educational administrators. Scholarships and loans to foreign students, international joint studies at universities and international networks are also provided.

Chapter 15. Changing Political Process of Education Policy

1. The Features and Changing of Japanese Education Policy Process

The policy process is usually affected by a lot of factors which involve education. There may be Ministry of Education, Sports, Science and Culture (MESSC), local boards of education, principals of various stages of schools, and teachers' unions as direct parties concerned. Politicians, political parties, the Ministry of Finance, business circles and mass media etc. also have a certain role in forming education policy. However, substantial influence does not belong to all parties equally. In the process of education policy, especially, Ministry of Education, Culture, Sports, Science and Technology (MEXT) and politicians in the Liberal Democracy party (LDP) which has had prominent power for a long time—have played critical roles so far. Members of Parliament (MPs) who are especially interested in education (often called "education zoku (group)" in Japan) within the LDP and highly ranked officials of Ministry of Education, Culture, Sports, Science and Technology are the most important actors. On the other hand, opposition parties and teachers' unions have not been given proper representation in that process.

This complicated relation among actors has continued until quite recently. However, such structure has been changing gradually from around 2000. When education reform was proposed by the leadership of the prime minister in the 1980's, the National Council on Education Reform (NCER) was organized under the Nakasone administration. This education reform aimed to transcend post-war education as standardized and realize the removal of restrictions on the school system while respecting individuality and the international society. But the ideas of these radical reforms by the prime minister and their advisers were not enough reflected in its final proposal.

Since 2000, education reforms of these targets have in fact been implemented by the leadership of the prime minister's office. In this chapter, such changing patterns of recent years are analyzed. (decision making process in MEXT and board of education described in Chapter 7 and 8, Part 2).

2. Education Policy Process under the LDP Government (1950s-1970s)

(1) Education policy and political process in Japan

Japan has the parliamentary cabinet system of government and the LDP (Japanese conservative party) was in power from 1955 to 1993 (1994–2009 and 2012–present). This party was integrated into one politically, so bills presented by the cabinet were rarely rejected by the Diet. Occasionally, some amendments were made or bills were obliged to withdraw because of serious conflicts between political parties or public opinion.

Bills presented to the Diet are approved by the Cabinet Council, but it is just a formality and the content of bills is usually examined by the government officials in advance.

The officials have substantial power in policy making process, but at the same time, they need to be supported by LDP MPs (Members of Parliament) to ensure their bills are approved by the Diet. From this point of view, officials and LDP MPs seem to depend on each other for their interests and in particular they keep very close relations with officials of MESSC and MPs who belong to the Education Zoku, which means Groups of MPs who are interested in specific fields and perform actively in policy-making process.

On the other hand, during this period, LDP governments needed agreements among the Executive Council and the Policy Affairs Research Council including the education branch of the LDP before submitting any bills to the cabinet. The pattern of decision making process in the LDP was called a bottom-up system and it contributed to getting consensus within the party anytime. In other words, this situation made it quite difficult to introduce radical changes in policy or to implement an intension of the prime minister such as the "top down" system. In particular, the zoku-group played a critical role in the decision making process (this often means they usually share the same interests between related actors in political communities). Education policies showed the same trends during that period.

(2) Political conflicts and consensus in education policy (1950-1970s)

From 1950s to 1980s, there were serious conflicts between the LDP government/Ministry of Education and the opposite side (socialist party, communist party and the teachers' union, etc.). As a result, left wing parties and the teachers' union were excluded from the decision making process regarding education policy.

However LDP politicians and Ministry of Education had not continued this process. Additionally, they had gradually moved away from the steamroller process in parliament and from that point of view, the LDP government is likely to compromise according to the views of the media, other parties, and public opinion are going. So was the case when the Fundamental Law of Education (FLE) was to be revised. The LDP government and Ministry of Education tended to avoid putting highly political risky issues on the agenda until the 2000s. In this sense, it seemed there was some degree of influence from the media, opposite party, and teacher's union indirectly affecting the education policy process.

3. Education Policy Process during 1970s-1980s and NCER
(1) Some elements of economic and social changes

In the 1970's, education became the target of criticism again, because it had failed to adjust to the economic development and maturation of society.

The business community also criticized general education in secondary and upper secondary school which could not supply able human resources for economic and industrial growth. The business community also asked to make it required that secondary and the higher education system be more diversified and more science oriented for its further development.

(2) NCER (1984-1986)

After the 1980's, high economic growth had begun to slow down and the government had to face financial reconstruction. In this context, administrative reform (this means curtailment of public sector organization) became an urgent undertaking.

In the US and the UK during the 1980s, governments introduced some new policies like quasi-market in public policies, privatization, and new public management and these policies have been accepted in other advanced countries including Japan.

The Nakasone administration started the reform of the administrative system and education. The newly launched NCER under the prime minister was the symbol of such direction. The target on the NCER by Nakasone and their advisers was to realize a more neo-liberal and international education than that of the post-war period.

This newly organized council, provided by the prime minister, was unique enough not to be affected by the zoku-group of the LDP and Ministry of Education. This type of Advisory Council was the first case and it became a model afterwards. However, this council didn't have its own staff and was obliged to depend on Ministry of Education officials. Nakasone' own idea to reform education had to face a compromise with the former affective actor, Ministry of Education. In fact, members of this council were mixed, from those with close ties to prime minister who insisted strongly on reform, to those with specialist of education against the radical reform.

As the result of this conflict, it could only propose a very limited liberalization of publicly provided school (for example, the introduction of credit-based upper secondary school and flexibility university entrance qualification), and maintained the present basic educational system which Nakasone's advisers strongly hoped to abolish.

4. Education Policy in the 21st Century

(1) Policy councils and changing style of decision-making

The most important factor in education policy in the 21st century is to utilize policy councils established by the prime minister's office.

There are many policy councils in education policy, the National Commission on Education Reform (NCER) by the Obuchi administration in 2000, the Council for Revitalization of Education (CRE) under the first Abe administration 2006, the CRE of the second Abe administration etc. As the prime minister and Chief Cabinet Secretary organized them and lead these policy councils, it is easy for the prime minister's intentions to directly affect education policy.

Members of these councils include the president, academic staff of universities, school teachers, superintendents, governors, ex-governors, writers, journalist, and people from sports and business activities.

On the contrary, members of the CCE under MEXT are comprised mainly of education specialists whose process and proposals are likely to be readily accepted as a plan for education. It has played a substantial role in the policy making of MEXT.

Although the Nakasone administration tried to realize the system led by the intentions of the prime minister directly in the 1980's as mentioned above, it could not be accomplished. However, in the case of newly launched council, members can be drawn widely from inside and outside education according to the prime minister's intentions and collectively, are able to affect to the entire process and proposals of the council.

(2) Policy councils and education policy

NCER (2000—2001) proposed some ideas, introducing choice of school, characteristic schools, 'community school', and diversifying patterns of entrance exams for universities and these proposals have been realized. At the same time it put forward conservative directions, for example, to encourage moral education, for schools to face bullying of children. Also, it proposed the revision of FLE and made the Basic Plan for the Promotion of Education.

Under the Obuchi administration the task for revising FLE started, and it was approved in 2006 under the first Abe administration. Such a process used to be unimaginable before 2000.

The second Abe administration (2012-) organized the CRE in 2013, to revive his first council. Its proposals have been implemented accordingly, to introduce moral education as a formal subject, to approve a new type school which connects lower secondary and upper secondary school, to revise the Law concerning Organization and Operation of Local Educational Administration (LCOOLEA) to let the local education committees and superintendents be more powerful, and to reform the university entrance examination system. This council under the first Abe administration also proposed the revision of Educational Personnel Certification Law and afterwards it was implemented as well.

(3) New decision making process in education policy

Recently, the basic decision making process as to education has shifted to the councils led by the prime minister's office, and actual and precise policies depend on the CCE under MEXT. The role of the prime minister for making education policies has become larger and also his advisers and other staff around him are likely to affect the education policy much more than ever. In other words, the traditional power of MEXT and education zoku has become smaller. This situation can be understood as the main reason in recent years for the complete change in how education policies are made.

5. The Changes and Problems of Education Policy Process in the 21st Century
(1) The decline and transformation of MEXT

The key feature of this changing pattern comes from increasing power of the prime minister's office as a whole. This also has brought a decline in the power of MEXT and education zoku. In addition, some other points can be noticed which made this change possible.

Recently, there is much more pressure to reduce the governmental budget and the Ministry of Finance has been the leading actor in this movement. Accordingly, MEXT has to depend on the MPs' power and the authority of the prime minister's office to resist this process and gradually MEXT tends to follow the decision making process of the prime minister's office.

(2) Political backgrounds

The reason why zoku group lost their power could be found in the reform of election system since 1994. As a result of this reform, the former system was replaced by a new single-seat constituency electoral system for the election of the House of Representatives. The proportional representative system was introduced at the same time, but the number of seats for the former was much more than the latter. And subsequently, this new election system strongly has affected Japanese politics.

Before the election system reform, the most important factor to win election is the personal ability of each candidate to organize people and to secure funds for their election campaign, rather than the power of one's political party, especially in the case of the conservative party. In such circumstances, plural candidates fought in one election district and sometimes cases when candidates who belonged to the same party could be observed running against each other, the LDP had two candidates in the same election districts. To win election, candidates of the LDP should depend on their own organization in that area rather than within the LDP itself.

The LDP is a party consisted of a coalition of individual politicians hence, the unity and cohesive power of the LDP is relatively weak as a whole. In such a situation, zoku group could have influential power in decision the making process for a long time. However after the new election system was introduced, the situation changed party politics dramatically, in particular for the LDP.

Under the new system, candidates are asked to be approved officially by the party. After this system started, the power of the executive of party increased and on the contrary the autonomy of individual politicians decreased. This situation affected the policy decision making process. The changing of the election system since 1994 has weakened the power of zoku group. Consequently the circumstance around the policy making process for education has completely changed and the power of the leaders of political parties and the prime minister's office has grown steadily.

(3) The problems and prospects on future

However, it still seems to be difficult to implement such reforms as diffusing the school choice system, promoting private cooperation to involve public education, and diversification of publicly provided schools etc. These policies have been criticized by actors concerning education e.g. school teachers, academic staff. The reasons of such difficulty are said to be implementation is likely to depend on the traditional way of resolving problems.

Actors related to education e.g. school teachers, academic staff, education officers, parents, etc. do not always share the same educational values proposed by the policy councils under the LDP government. There is distrust and different opinions among academic staff and teachers against the proposals of policy councils.

Teachers and local boards of education tend to respect the conventional pattern of policy making and also there are huge gaps of cognition between central and local government, and schools. In the process of implementing policy, teachers and boards of education tend to interpret governmental policy based on their own views. This is the so-called problem of "street-level bureaucracy". It is so hard to implement policy perfectly according to the course set by the government, especially when there is a disagreement between policy-makers and actors in schools.

Compared with the circumstances before 2000, these days it has become easier to decide policy quickly and directly according to the intentions of the prime minister and his advisers. But as far as the huge gaps of values and cognition among actors in education, these reforms could be left as political issues.

Statistics

Further Readings

Chronology

Useful Website

Statistics

1. Present School System (2017)

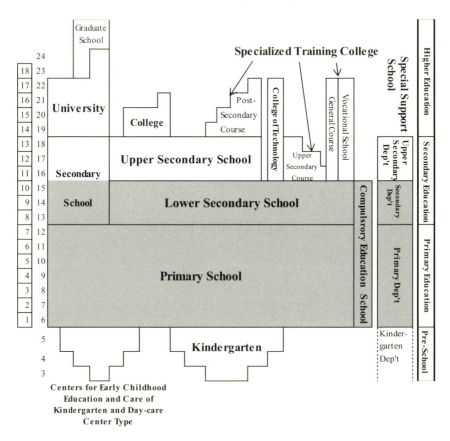

2. Number of Students, Students and Full-time Teachers (2016)

Table 1: Pre-school Education (Ch.1-1)

School Types	Sector	Schools	Students	Full-time Teachers		
				Male	Female	Total
Kindergarten	National	49	5,934	45	296	341
	Public	4,127	223,066	844	19,831	20,675
	Private	7,076	1,111,301	5,618	73,323	78,941
	Total	11,252	1,339,761	6,507	93,450	99,957
Centers for Early Childhood Education a nd Care *	National	—	—	—	—	—
	Public	452	52,012	257	6,757	7,014
	Private	2,370	345,575	2,869	47,235	50,104
	Total	2,822	397,857	3,126	53,992	57,118
Day-care Center etc.	Day-care	26,237	2,393,988	n/a	n/a	n/a
	Regional	3,879	39,895	n/a	n/a	n/a
	Total	30,116	2,433,883	n/a	n/a	n/a

* Kindergarten and Day-care Center types only

Table 2: Primary and Secondary Education (Ch.1-1, Ch.1-2, Ch11)

School Types	Sector	Schools	Students	Full-time Teachers		
				Male	Female	Total
Primary School	National	72	39,543	1,169	664	1,833
	Public	20,011	6,366,785	153,722	256,394	410,116
	Private	230	77,187	2,443	2,581	5,024
	Total	20,313	6,483,515	157,334	259,639	416,973
Unified Secondary School	National	73	30,840	1,100	541	1,641
	Public	9,555	3,133,644	133,190	102,033	235,233
	Private	776	241,545	9,369	5,745	15,114
	Total	10,404	3,406,029	143,659	108,319	251,978
Compulsory Education School	National	—	—	—	—	—
	Public	22	12,702	430	504	934
	Private	—	—	—	—	—
	Total	22	12,702	430	504	934

Table 3: Secondary Education (Ch.1-3, 5, Ch.12)

School Types	Sector	Schools	Students	Full-time Teachers		
				Male	Female	Total
Upper Secondary School	National	15	8,630	403	178	581
	Public	3,589	2,252,942	116,468	56,273	172,741
	Private	1,321	1,047,770	43,445	17,844	61,289
	Total	4,925	3,309,342	160,316	74,295	234,611
Unified Secondary School	National	4	3,107	124	87	211
	Public	31	21,941	1,053	608	1,661
	Private	17	7,380	494	190	684
	Total	52	32,428	1,671	995	2,556
Special Support School	National	45	2,991	723	798	1,521
	Public	1,067	136,072	31,121	49,437	80,558
	Private	13	758	143	150	293
	Total	1,125	139,821	31,987	50,385	82,372

Table 4: Higher education (Ch.1-4, Ch.13)

School Types	Sector	Schools	Students	Full-time Teachers		
				Male	Female	Total
University	National	86	610,401	54,233	10,538	64,771
	Public	91	150,513	9,508	3,786	13,294
	Private	600	2,112,710	76,784	29,399	106,183
	Total	777	2,873,624	140,525	43,723	184,248
College	National	—	—	—	—	—
	Public	17	6,750	272	213	485
	Private	324	121,710	3,621	4,034	7,655
	Total	341	128,460	3,893	4,247	8,140
College of Technology	National	51	51,623	3,445	386	3,831
	Public	3	3,740	272	27	299
	Private	3	2,295	135	19	154
	Total	57	57,658	3,852	432	4,284

3. The Transition of Enrollment Rates and Number of Schools

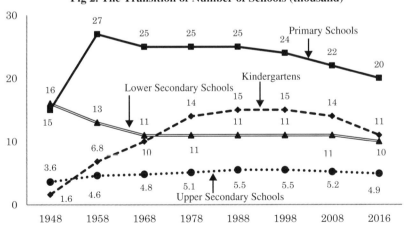

Fig 1. The transition of enrollment rates

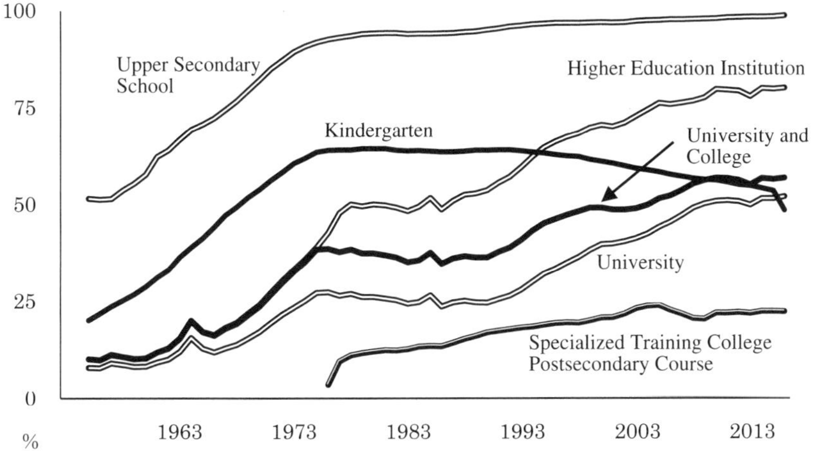

(As the enrollment rates of primary and lower secondary school have been more than 99% of this period, they are not shown in this figure.)

Fig 2. The Transition of Number of Schools (thousand)

4. The Age Distribution of Teachers (2013)

Figure 3. The Age Distribution of Kindergarten Teachers

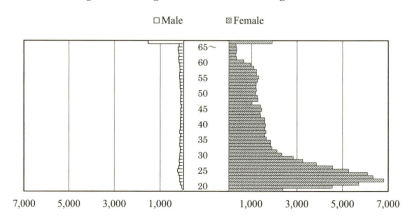

Figure 4. The Age Distribution of Primary School Teachers

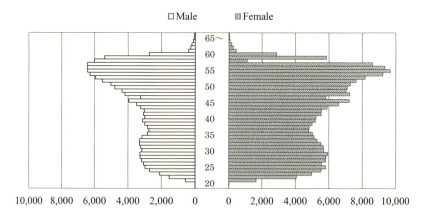

Figure 5. The Age Distribution of Lower Secondary School Teachers

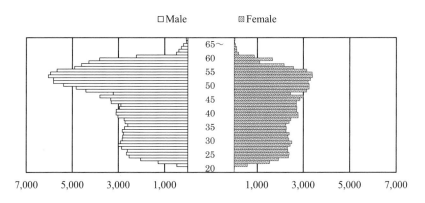

Figure 6. The Age Distribution of Upper Secondary School Teachers

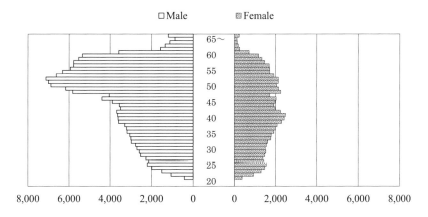

234

Further Readings

Educational Administration

• Yaichi WAKAI (Editorial Supervisor), Kazukiyo KOHNO (Editor), Shigeru TAKAMI (Editor), Makoto YUKI (Editor), *Six Laws of Required Teaching <2017edition>* (in Japanese), Kyodo-shuppan, Tokyo, 2016.

• Shigeru TAKAMI (Editor), Kenji HATTORI (Editor), *Educational Administration Proposal (Heisei Edition)* (in Japanese), Kyodo-shuppan, Tokyo, 2016.

• Akiyoshi YONEZAWA (Commentator), OECD (Editor), Rie MORI (Translator), *OECD Reviews of Tertiary Education: JAPAN* (in Japanese), Organization for Economic Co-operation and Development, Paris, and Asashi Shoten, Tokyo, 2009.

<Chapter 3>

• Japanese Association for the Study of Educational Administration, *Educational Administration and Management in Japan* (in Japanese), Cengage Learning Asia, Tokyo, 2008.

• Hiromichi OJIMA.et.al, *Historical Changes and School Management Reform* (in Japanese), Gakubun-sha, Tokyo, 2007.

• Kiyoaki SHINOHARA, *Jurisprudence for Education* (in Japanese), Minerva-shobo, Kyoto, 2013.

<Chapter 5>

• Manabu UEDA, *Private Schools in Japan and United Kingdom* (in Japanese), Tamagawa University Press, Tokyo, 2009.

• Makoto YUKI, *Japanese Constitution and Private School Education* (in Japanese), Kyodo-Shuppan, Tokyo, 2014.

<Chapter 7>

- Nobutomo HIGUCHI, *An Overview of Educational Administration and Finance: The Structure and Issues of Contemporary Public Education System* (in Japanese), Meisei University Press, Tokyo, 2007.
- Haruyoshi HIRAHARA, *Introduction to Educational Administration Studies* (in Japanese), University of Tokyo Press, Tokyo, 2009.
- Yuji IBUKA et al, *Education and Educational Administration* (in Japanese), Keiso-shobo, Tokyo, 2015.
- Fumio ISODA, *Educational Administration: Toward the Independent and Cooperative Society* (in Japanese), Gyosei, Tokyo, 2006.
- Fumio ISODA, *Educational Administration: Toward the Sharing Community* (in Japanese), Minerva-shobo, Kyoto, 2014.
- Masaaki KATUNO & Norihiro FUJIMOTO, *Educational Administration Studies* (in Japanese), Gakubun-sha, Tokyo, 2015.
- Masayoshi KIYOHARA, Kaori SUETOMI, Manami HONZU, *Education and System in Japan From the Perspective of Fundamental Law of Education: What to Be Changed by the Revised Law?* (in Japanese), Kyodo-shuppan, Tokyo, 2008.
- Shigehisa KOMATSU, *Where Does the School Reform Go?: Reality, Reform, and Challenges of Educational Administration and School Management* (in Japanese), Showado, Kyoto, 2005.
- Shigehisa KOMATSU, *Educational Administration: The Future Map of Educational Governance* (in Japanese), Showado, Kyoto, 2013.
- Kazukiyo KOHNO, *Educational Administration Studies* (in Japanese), Minerva-shobo, Kyoto, 2014.
- Yokuo MURATA & Misturu YAMAGUTI, *A BILINGUAL TEXT – Education in Contemporary Japan: System and Content*, Toshindo, Tokyo, 2010.
- Hiroshi SHIONO, *Administrative Law III: Administrative Organization Act* (in Japanese), Yuhikaku, Tokyo, 2008.
- Shigeru WATANABE, *Educational Administration* (in Japanese), Nihon Tosho Center, Tokyo, 2004.

• Toshiro YOKOI, *Educational Administration Studies: For the Future of Children and the Youth* (in Japanese), Yachiyo-shuppan, Tokyo, 2014.

Examination for Japanese University Admission for International Students
• Japan Student Services Organization, *Examination Guide for Examination for Japanese University Admission for International Students (With Application Document) <For Domestic Examination>* (in Japanese), Sanpou, Tokyo, 2017.
• Education For The Future, *International Student Special Admission Issue Collection for National Universities* (in Japanese),Senmon-kyoiku, Tokyo, 2015.

Japanese Language
• Japan Student Services Organization, *2016 Examination for Japanese University Admission for International Students (1st Session)* (in Japanese), Bonjin-sha, Tokyo, 2016.
• Academic Japanese Group, *Japanese for International College/ Graduate Students* (in Japanese), Alc press, Tokyo, 2015.
• Japanese Educational Exchanges and Services, *Japanese Language Proficiency Test (N1~N5)* (in Japanese), Bonjin-sha, Tokyo, 2012.
• 3a Network, *Minna no Nihongo* (in Japanese),3a Network, Tokyo, 2012.
• Kei ISHIGURO, Chie TSUTSUI, *Rules of Important Sentence Expression for International Students* (in Japanese), 3a Network, Tokyo, 2009.
• Kiyokata KATO, *BJT Business Japanese Proficiency Test Official Guide(Planation and Practice Test Including CD)* (in Japanese), The Japan Kanji Aptitude Testing Foundation, Kyoto, 2009.
• Nobuko NITSU, Fujiko SATO, *How to Write Logical Sentences for International Students* (in Japanese), 3a Network, Tokyo, 2003.

Chronology

AD	Japanese Calendar	Education related Legislations and Events
1946	Showa 21	• Constitution of Japan enacted (implemented from following year)
1947	22	• FLE, SEL enacted • First Course of Study released • Foundation of Japan Teachers' Union • Foundation of Japan University Accreditation Association • Child Welfare Act
1948	23	• Board of Education Law
1949	24	• Old university system turned into new university system • Educational Personnel Certification Act • Special Act for Education Personnel • Private Schools Act • Social Education Law
1951	26	• Act on Promotion of Vocational Education • Inauguration of University Entrance Qualification Examination • Course of Study revised.
1952	27	• Foundation of CCE • "Popolo" Incident of Tokyo University (Decided 1963)
1953	28	• Kyoto Asahigaoka Lower Secondary School incident (to 1954) • Science Education Promotion Act • Act on the Promotion of the Part-time and Correspondence Education at High Schools
1954	29	• The Act for Partial Amendment of Special Act for Education Personnel • Act on Temporary Measures concerning Assurance of Political • Neutrality of Education of Compulsory Education Schools (two Education Laws)
1956	31	• Act on the Organization and Operation of Local Educational Administration • Enactment of University Establishment Standards • Establishment of the Science and Technology Agency

1956	31	• Establishment of the Science and Technology Agency • Inauguration of national achievement tests(to 1965) • Course of Study revised(high school only)
1958	33	• Act on Standards for Class Formation and Fixed Number of School Personnel of Public Compulsory Education Schools
1961	36	• Asahikawa Achievement Test Case(Decided 1976) • Free textbook fight in Nagahama, Kochi (Decided 1964) • Act on Appropriate Location, Standards for Fixed Number of School Personnel and Other Matters Related to Public High Schools • Course of Study revised.
1962	37	• Inauguration of Colleges of Technology
1963	38	• Textbooks of compulsory education became free of charge.
1965	40	• The Ienaga Textbook Court Cases (Decided 1997)
1968	43	• Establishment of Agency for Cultural Affairs
1969	44	• Cancellation of the entrance exam of Tokyo University for massive student movement.
1971	46	• CCE released 46 report • Kojimachi Lower Secondary School Report Case (Decided 1988) • Course of Study revised.
1974	49	• Enrollment rate of high school surpassed 90 percent.
1975	50	• Act on Subsidies for Private Schools
1976	51	• Inauguration of Specialized Training College
1978	53	• Inauguration of the Joint First-Stage Achievement Test (to 1989)
1980	55	• Course of Study revised.
1983	58	• Foundation of the Open University of Japan
1984	59	• Establishment of National Council on Educational Reform (to 1987)
1988	63	• Social Education Bureau at Ministry of Education, Science and Culture turned into Lifelong Learning Bureau • Inauguration of induction trainings for newly appointed teachers • Inauguration of credit-based high schools

1990	Heisei 2	• Inauguration of National Center Test for University Entrance for University
1991	3	• Deregulation of University Establishment Standards; Foundation of National Institution for Academic Degrees • Establishment of All Japan Teachers and Staff Union
1992	4	• Five-day week system partly implemented for schools • Course of Study revised.
1998	10	• Inauguration of a unified lower-upper secondary education at public schools • Curriculum Council proposed relaxed education (a.k.a. Yutori Education).
1999	11	• Act on National Flag and Anthem
2000	12	• Establishment of the National Commission on Educational • Reform; Inauguration of Period for Integrated Studies • Inauguration of School Council System • Deregulation of qualification for principal and head teacher • Clarification of the position and function of staff meeting
2001	13	• MESSC and Technology Agency integrated into Ministry of Education, Culture, Sports, Science and Technology(MEXT) • Ministry of Health and Welfare and Ministry of Labor integrated into Ministry of Health, Labor and Welfare (MHLW).
2002	14	• Five-day week system completely implemented for schools • Course of Study revised.
2004	16	• National universities turned into National University Corporation • Inauguration of the School Management Council system.
2005	17	• Central Government's Share of Compulsory Education Expenses reduced from 1/2 to 1/3 • University Entrance Qualification Examination abolished and Upper Secondary School Equivalency Examination started • Act on Support for Persons with Developmental Disabilities
2006	18	• Amendment of FLE • Inauguration of Centers for Early Childhood Education and Care • Establishment of Education Rebuilding Council (ERC)

2007	19	• Amendment Three Education Laws 1. SEL: Inauguration of vice-principal, senior teacher, advanced skill teacher 2. Act on the Organization and Operation of Local Educational Administration: Clarification of responsibility of Board of Education 3. The Act for Partial Amendment of Educational Personnel Certification Act and Special Act for Education Personnel • Inauguration of Teacher Certification Renewal System) • Inauguration of National assessment of academic ability • Inauguration of Professional Schools for Teacher Education • School for the Blind, School for the Deaf and School for the Disabled integrated into Special Support School.
2008	20	• Foreign language activities implemented for primary schools.
2011	23	• Bullying and suicide incident at a lower secondary school student in Otsu city • Textbook adoption issue in Yaeyama, Okinawa • Course of Study revised.
2013	25	• Establishment of Council for Revitalization of Education (CRE) • Act for the Measures to Prevent Bullying
2015	27	• Inauguration of new Board of Education system • Inauguration of the Comprehensive Support System for Children and Child-rearing • Foundation of Japan Sports Agency • Inauguration of Compulsory Education School
2016	28	• Inauguration of Compulsory Education School

Useful Website

- Cabinet Office, Government Of Japan : CAO
  http://www.cao.go.jp/index-e.html
- Ministry of Education, Culture, Sports, Science and Technology : MEXT
  http://www.mext.go.jp/en/index.htm
- Ministry of Foreign Affairs : MOFA (VISA / Residing in Japan)
  http://www.mofa.go.jp/j_info/visit/visa/index.html
- Ministry of Justice : MOJ (Japanese Law Translation)
  http://www.japaneselawtranslation.go.jp/?re=02
- National Institute for Educational Policy Research : NIER
  http://www.nier.go.jp/English/index.html
- Immigration Bureau of JAPAN (Entry Procedures)
  http://www.immi-moj.go.jp/english/index.html
- Independent Administrative Institution Japan Student Services Organization : JASSO
  http://www.jasso.go.jp/en/index.html
- Association for the Promotion of Japanese Language Education (Search for Japanese language school)
  http://www.nisshinkyo.org/search/index_e.html
- Study in Japan Comprehensive Guide
  http://www.studyjapan.go.jp/en/index.html
- Japanese Language Proficiency Test : JLPT
  http://www.jlpt.jp/e/index.html

Index

absenteeism （不登校）	184, 185, 188, 191, 192
accountability （アカウンタビリティ）	168, 179
active learning （アクティブ・ラーニング）	44, 46, 50, 60, 204
approval of textbook （教科書検定）	80
Basic Plan for Promotion of Education （教育振興基本計画）	206, 222
birth rate （出生率）	18–, 44, 58, 116, 179, 203, 205–, 211
bullying （いじめ）	33, 38, 139, 148, 152, 188, 191–, 222
career education （キャリア教育）	49, 199
Central Council for Education （CCE）（中央教育審議会）	65, 92–, 106–, 135, 148, 174, 176, 187, 195, 199–, 212, 221–
Central government share of compulsory education expense （義務教育費国庫負担金）	164
college of technology （高等専門学校）	53, 55
community learning center （Kominkan）（公民館）	117–, 120, 124
community school （コミュニティ・スクール）	93, 94, 221
Constitution of Japan （日本国憲法）	16, 19, 24, 32, 76, 79–, 110, 115, 117, 154, 172–
Council for Revitalization of Education (CRE: 2013–)（教育再生実行会議）	131, 148, 176, 187, 221–
Course of Study （学習指導要領）	35, 37, 44, 48–, 50–, 67, 77–, 80, 111, 130, 178, 213–
curriculum management （カリキュラム・マネジメント）	29, 79, 81–
decentralization （地方分権）	124, 140, 165, 170–, 174, 190
Decentralization Acts （地方分権一括法）	137–, 145, 157

education for international understanding（国際理解教育）	169, 212–
extra-curricular activity (→ special activity)（特別活動）	19, 51, 77, 197, 213–
extra-curricular clubs（部活動）	44, 193–
foreign language activities（外国語活動）	35–, 77, 210–
foreign language education（外国語教育）	210–
globalization（地球一体化）	58, 198, 203, 205–
governor（知事）	112–, 142, 146, 171, 176, 179–, 221
grade 7-gap（中一ギャップ）	188
head of local government（地方自治体の首長）	150–, 157
head teacher（主任）	89
incorporated educational institutions (IEI)（学校法人）	33, 43, 84, 97, 109–, 112–
Information & Communication Technology (ICT)（情報通信技術）	21, 39, 106, 153, 202
in-service training（現職研修）	99, 102, 104–, 205, 215–
internationalization（国際化）	20, 58, 208, 210, 212
layman control（素人による統制）	144, 150
lifelong learning（生涯学習）	117, 123, 125, 127, 133, 135, 203
mayor（市長）	146, 172, 176, 179–
moral education（道徳教育）	35–, 46, 77–, 214, 222
National Assessment of Academic Ability（全国学力・学習状況調査）	37, 156
National Center Test for University Admission (NCTUA)（大学入学センター試験）	55–, 200
National Commission on Education Reform (NCER:2000-2001)（教育改革国民会議）	221
National Council on Education Reform (NCER: 1984-87)（臨時教育審議会）	176, 212, 217
nursery center（保育園）	25–, 152

Parent Teacher Association（PTA）	95, 125
PDCA cycle（PDCAサイクル）	81, 90–, 167
period for integrated study（総合的な学習の時間）	35, 78, 213–
principal（校長）	44, 68, 76, 81, 84, 87–, 99–, 101–, 113, 122, 156, 169, 187, 189, 217
professional leadership (board of education)（専門職による指導）	144, 150
Programme for International Students Assessment (PISA)（OECD生徒の学習到達度調査）	18, 37
public nature（公の性質）	97, 109, 113
public opinion（世論）	16, 123, 145, 148, 179, 218–
scholarship（奨学金）	61, 74, 216
school attendance zone（通学区域、学区）	33
school evaluation（学校評価）	91
school management council（学校運営協議会）	90, 93–, 95, 185
school meal（学校給食）	19, 52, 153
6-3 system（6-3制）	130, 185, 187
special activity (→ extra-curricular activity) 特別活動	35–, 38, 44, 51
specialized training college（専門学校）	53–, 70–
supervisor（指導主事）	171, 177, 180
textbook adoption（教科書採択）	81
TOKKATSU → special activity（特別活動）	51
tuition（授業料）	19, 32, 61–, 110, 116, 167, 197
unified primary & lower secondary school education（小中一貫校）	186–
vocational education（職業教育）	48–, 54, 73–
work overload of teachers（教員の過重労働）	194
zest for living（生きる力）	34, 37, 78, 200, 213–

Editor's Postscript

This edition was planned, firstly, to celebrate our 60th anniversary of our Society, and secondly, to revise the last edition published in 1999. In this context, this committee was organized in the spring of 2016, and the meeting for the contributors was held in autumn of the same year. The editorial committee is so proud that more than thirty members of our society have been cooperative and contributed this publication and our acknowledgement should be given to all of them. The final Japanese papers by them were accepted at the second half of April and the English version was also prepared by them simultaneously. The precise checking was undertaken over and over and finally this book was successfully launched recently.

In recent years, a huge number of visitors come to Japan and vice versa, so many Japanese people are going abroad for varying lengths of stay. From this, the committee noticed that so many people, whether in their country or in Japan, are interested in economic growth, technology, and also Japanese thinking or culture etc. At the same time it is only natural that a number of people from abroad have become interested in education as the base of Japanese society. We hope that this book can be helpful to people who are interested in the facts concerning education.

Two photos (p.17, 24) were taken by the author of that chapter, and others were presented by the Compact Disk ('Educational System and School Activities', 2005) of the Center for Research for International Corporation and Educational Development (CRICED), University of Tsukuba.

Lastly, we would like to express our gratitude to Mr. Kent Hatashita for checking the English during intervals snatched from work at Senri Kinran University.

Chief editor UEDA, Manabu
Staff   MURATA, Yokuo
TANIGAWA, Yoshitaka
NAMBU, Hatsuyo
Secretary MIYAMURA, Yuko

JAPANESE EDUCATIONAL SYSTEM AND ITS ADMINISTRATION

The Kansai Society for Educational Administration (KSEA)

日本の教育制度と教育行政（英語版）

2018 年 3 月 31 日　　初版 第 1 刷発行　　　　　　　〔検印省略〕

定価はカバーに表示してあります。

編者　Ⓒ関西教育行政学会／発行者 下田勝司　　　　印刷・製本／中央精版印刷

東京都文京区向丘1-20-6　　郵便振替00110-6-37828

〒113-0023　TEL (03) 3818-5521　FAX (03) 3818-5514

発 行 所
株式 東信堂
会社

Published by TOSHINDO PUBLISHING CO., LTD.

1-20-6, Mukougaoka, Bunkyo-ku, Tokyo, 113-0023, Japan
E-mail : tk203444@fsinet.or.jp http://www.toshindo-pub.com

ISBN978-4-7989-1495-4 C3037

Ⓒ関西教育行政学会

東信堂

ネオリベラル期教育の思想と構造 —書き換えられた教育の原理	福田誠治	六二〇〇円
アメリカ公立学校の社会史 —コモンスクールからNCLB法まで	W・J・リース著／小川佳万・浅沼茂監訳	四六〇〇円
アメリカ 間違いがまかり通っている時代 —公立学校の企業型改革への批判と解決法	D・ラヴィッチ著／末藤美津子訳	三八〇〇円
教育による社会的正義の実現 —アメリカの挑戦（1945-1980）	D・ラヴィッチ著／末藤美津子訳	五六〇〇円
学校改革抗争の100年 —20世紀アメリカ教育史	D・ラヴィッチ著／末藤・宮本・佐藤訳	六四〇〇円
現代学力テスト批判 —実態調査・思想・認識論からのアプローチ	北野秋男・小川佳人・小笠原喜康編	二七〇〇円
ポストドクター —若手研究者養成の現状と課題	北野秋男	三六〇〇円
日本のティーチング・アシスタント制度 —大学教育の改善と人的資源の活用	北野秋男編著	二八〇〇円
現代アメリカの教育アセスメント行政の展開 —マサチューセッツ州（MCASテスト）を中心に	北野秋男編	四八〇〇円
アメリカ公民教育におけるサービス・ラーニング	唐木清志	四六〇〇円
【増補版】現代アメリカにおける学力形成論の展開 —スタンダードに基づくカリキュラムの設計	石井英真	四六〇〇円
アメリカにおける多文化的歴史カリキュラムの現代的展開	桐谷正信	三六〇〇円
アメリカにおける学校認証評価の現代的展開	浜田博文編著	二八〇〇円
ハーバード・プロジェクト・ゼロの芸術認知理論とその実践 —創造的知性とクリエティビティを育むハワード・ガードナーの教育戦略	池内慈朗	六五〇〇円
現代教育制度改革への提言 上・下　日本教育制度学会編		各二八〇〇円
日本の教育をどうデザインするか	村田翼夫編著	二八〇〇円
現代日本の教育課題 —二一世紀の方向性を探る	岩槻知也編著	三六〇〇円
日本の教育制度と教育行政（英語版）　関西教育行政学会編		二五〇〇円
バイリンガルテキスト現代日本の教育	村田翼夫編著	三八〇〇円
人格形成概念の誕生 —近代アメリカの教育概念史	山口満編著	三六〇〇円
社会性概念の構築 —アメリカ進歩主義教育の概念史	田中智志	三八〇〇円
グローバルな学びへ —協同と刷新の教育	田中智志	二〇〇〇円
学びを支える活動へ —存在論の深みから	田中智志編著	二〇〇〇円
社会形成力育成カリキュラムの研究	西村公孝	六五〇〇円

〒113-0023　東京都文京区向丘1-20-6　TEL 03-3818-5521　FAX 03-3818-5514　振替 00110-6-37828
Email tk203444@fsinet.or.jp　URL:http://www.toshindo-pub.com/

※定価：表示価格（本体）＋税